MEXICAN-AMERICAN CUISINE

THE ILAN STAVANS LIBRARY OF LATINO CIVILIZATION

MEXICAN-AMERICAN CUISINE

Edited by Ilan Stavans

GREENWOOD

AN IMPRINT OF ABC-CLIO, LLC
Santa Barbara, California • Denver, Colorado • Oxford, England

Library of Congress Cataloging-in-Publication Data

Mexican-American cuisine / edited by Ilan Stavans.
    p. cm. — (The Ilan Stavans library of Latino civilization)
 ISBN 978-0-313-35822-7 (hard back : alk. paper) — ISBN 978-0-313-35823-4 (e-book)
1. Cooking, American—Southwestern style. 2. Mexican American cooking.
3. Hispanic Americans—Social life and customs. I. Stavans, Ilan.
TX715.2.S69M476 2011
394.1'208968073—dc23
                              2011023214

ISBN: 978-0-313-35822-7
EISBN: 978-0-313-35823-4

15 14 13 12 11   1 2 3 4 5

This book is also available on the World Wide Web as an eBook.
Visit www.abc-clio.com for details.

Greenwood
An Imprint of ABC-CLIO, LLC

ABC-CLIO, LLC
130 Cremona Drive, P.O. Box 1911
Santa Barbara, California 93116-1911

This book is printed on acid-free paper ∞
Manufactured in the United States of America

CONTENTS

Series Foreword

The book series *The Ilan Stavans Library of Latino Civilization,* the first of its kind, is devoted to exploring all the facets of Hispanic civilization in the United States, with its ramifications in the Americas, the Caribbean Basin, and the Iberian Peninsula. The objective is to showcase its richness and complexity from a myriad perspective. According to the U.S. Census Bureau, the Latino minority is the largest in the nation. It is also the fifth largest concentration of Hispanics on the globe.

Out of every seven Americans, one traces his or her roots to the Spanish-speaking world. Mexicans make about 65 percent of the minority. Other major national groups are Puerto Ricans, Cubans, Dominicans, Ecuadorians, Guatemalans, Nicaraguans, Salvadorans, and Colombians. They are either immigrants, descendants of immigrants, or dwellers in a territory (Puerto Rico, the Southwest) having a conflicted relationship with the mainland United States. As such, they are the perfect example of *encuentro*: an encounter with different social and political modes, an encounter with a new language, and an encounter with a different way of dreaming.

The series is a response to the limited resources available and the abundance of stereotypes, which are a sign of lazy thinking. The twentieth-century Spanish philosopher José Ortega y Gasset, author of *The Revolt of the Masses,* once said: "By speaking, by thinking, we undertake to clarify things, and that forces us to exacerbate them, dislocate them, schematize them. Every concept is in itself an exaggeration." The purpose of the series is not to clarify but to complicate our understanding of Latinos. Do so many individuals from different national, geographic, economic, religious, and ethnic backgrounds coalesce as an integrated whole? Is there an *unum* in the *pluribus*?

Baruch Spinoza believed that every thing in the universe wants to persevere in its present form: a tree wants to be a tree, and a dog a dog. Latinos in the United States want to be Latinos in the United States—no easy task, and therefore an intriguing one to explore. Each volume of the series contains an assortment of approximately a dozen articles, essays, and interviews never gathered together before by journalists and specialists in their respective fields, followed by a bibliography of important resources of the topic. Their compilation is designed to generate debate and foster research: to complicate our knowledge. Every attempt is made to balance the ideological viewpoint of the authors. The target audience is students, specialists, and lay readers. Themes will range from politics to sports, from music to cuisine. Historical periods and benchmarks like the Mexican War, the Spanish American War, the Zoot Suit Riots, the Bracero Program, and the Cuban Revolution, as well as controversial topics like immigration, bilingual education, and Spanglish, will be tackled.

Democracy is only able to thrive when it engages in an open, honest transaction of information. By offering diverse, insightful volumes about Hispanic life in the United States and inviting people to engage in critical thinking, *The Ilan Stavans Library of Latino Civilization* seeks to open new vistas to appreciate the fastest growing, increasingly heterogeneous minority in the nation—to be part of the *encuentro*.

Illan Stavans

Introduction

Not long ago, I read a survey that suggested—emphatically, I recall—that in the late 1990s salsa replaced ketchup as America's favorite condiment. I have my doubts. Still, the sheer idea is inviting. As the unavoidable companion of nachos, tacos, and quesadillas, among other dishes, salsa is everywhere on north-of-the-border tables. Indeed, Mexican food is the fastest-growing ethnic cuisine in the country. In the area where I live, Amherst, Massachusetts, there are more Mexican restaurants than most other national foods combined.

When seen against the backdrop of Latino immigration, the irony, of course, is unavoidable: just as *mexicanos* are derided as unwelcome guests in the U.S. media, accused of stealing away jobs, their cookery reaches unforeseen levels of popularity. Wetback, go home! But not before you teach us to eat more adventurously …

Needless to say, Mexican and Mexican-American foods aren't the same. In fact, they are quite different. A Mexican will remind you that a burrito isn't really a wrap but a small donkey and that a margarita is a flower not a drink.

The present sampler—following the strict menu of *platillos principales* and *postres*—offers a sideboard of anthropological, ethnographic, sociological, and culinary disquisitions on Mexican cuisine. It then moves to the main dishes: an attempt at establishing the boundaries by Jeffrey M. Pilcher between Mexican and Mexican-American food, a topic continued by Helen Simons in her essay. It is followed by Kent Ian Paterson's focus on the battles over chile, a topic that novelist Laura Esquivel picks up from a belletristic perspective. Meredith E. Abarca offers some philosophical insights into the art of Mexican cuisine. There is also a piece by Frederick Trowbridge and Fernando Mendoza on obesity among Mexican-American children and adolescents, where the index of diabetics is the highest in the nation when compared to other age groups.

The volume concludes with the deserts: a handful of recipes and recommendations by nineteenth-century California chef Encarnación Pinedo, as well as impressionistic comments by journalist Camilo José Vergara and novelist Dagoberto Gilb. *¡Buen apetito!*

PART I
PLATILLOS PRINCIPALES

Tex-Mex, Cal-Mex, New Mex, or Whose Mex? Notes on the Historical Geography of Southwestern Cuisine

Jeffrey M. Pilcher

Residents of the United States often have a peculiar view of Mexican food, drawn more from Mexican American restaurants or from fast food simulations than from actual experience south of the border. While the combination plates at local restaurants offer little of the rich complexity of Mexico's regional cuisines, they do have a history of their own, one that reflects the ongoing struggle of Mexican Americans to gain acceptance and citizenship in the United States.[1]

The cooking of the Southwest, like Mexican cooking in general, embodies a fusion of Native American and Hispanic influences, the legacy of three centuries of first Spanish and then Mexican rule. As examples of a common regional style, *norteño* cooking, the dishes from different parts of the borderlands—resemble each other more than they do the foods of other parts of Mexico. One distinctive characteristic of northern Mexican cooking is the use of wheat flour instead of corn in making tortillas. The great herds of livestock raised along the frontier made norteños more carnivorous, in particular more fond of beef, than Mexicans farther south. On the other hand, the grassy plains and arid deserts of the north, well suited to cattle ranching and irrigated wheat farming, offered less variety in vegetables, herbs, and chiles, limiting the potential for complex sauces and soups. These common elements notwithstanding, considerable variety also exists within Southwestern cooking. Cheryl Alters Jamison and Bill Jamison, in their authoritative work, *The Border Cookbook*, define four broad regions straddling the U.S.–Mexican border: Texas and northeastern Mexico, New Mexico, Sonora, and California. This essay will describe these differing cooking styles from a historical and geographical perspective.[2]

Jeffrey M. Pilcher, "Tex-Mex, Cal-Mex, New Mex, or Whose Mex? Notes on the Historical Geography of Southwestern Cuisine," first published in *Journal of the Southwest* Vol. 43, No. 4, 2001. Used with permission of the *Journal of the Southwest*.

Native Americans and Hispanics in the Southwest already had long-established culinary traditions in 1848, when Mexico surrendered California, Arizona, New Mexico, and Texas to the United States in the Treaty of Guadalupe Hidalgo. The predominantly male fortune seekers who migrated to the region alternately looked down on the racially mixed residents and married into the more European-appearing elite, while grabbing land and wealth on an equal opportunity basis. A peculiar gender dynamic emerged in which Anglo newcomers feminized the male inhabitants—think of stereotypes of passive Mexican men in dress-like serapes and big, gaudy sombreros—and sexualized the women as "hot tamales" and "chili queens." In this contentious environment, the women's work of cooking and the traditionally male task of grilling meat became sites of cultural conflict and accommodation. Simultaneously attracted to and repelled by the piquant stews of Hispanic women in San Antonio, Anglo males ultimately appropriated chili by taming the hot peppers into a mass-produced and easily regulated powder. Outsiders found some Mexican American dishes simply repulsive, most notably menudo (tripe), thereby making them powerful symbols of ethnic identity. Between these two extremes, most Southwestern dishes gradually entered the mestizo stew that makes up the cuisine of the United States, acquiring new tastes and forms but maintaining clear links to their ethnic origins.[3]

CORN MOTHERS AND ANIMAL SPIRITS

For more than a thousand years, cooks of the Southwest have taken inspiration from the civilizations of Mesoamerica. The agricultural complex of maize, beans, and squash, domesticated in central Mexico, gradually diffused through much of North America in the first millennium of the Common Era. The staple tortilla—made by simmering maize in mineral lime (CaO), grinding it into *masa* (dough) on a *metate* (grinding stone), putting it into a flat round shape, and cooking it briefly on a griddle—had also begun to arrive in the Southwest before the Spaniards, as had the more elaborate tamales, dumplings made of the same dough steamed in cornhusks. Justifiably proud of their elaborate cuisine, the inhabitants of the Valley of Mexico dismissed their northern neighbors contemptuously as Chichimecas (dog-people) for their scavenging ways. Nevertheless, the lack of large domesticated animals reduced even the haughty warriors of the Aztec Empire to considerable hunting and gathering to supplement their basically vegetarian diet, thus belying some of their claims to superiority over cooks from the northern frontier.

An assortment of wild plants and animals formed the common basis for human subsistence in the Southwest. With its large size and savory meat, the deer stood out as the favorite game animal for much of North America, although Indians hunted smaller game as well, including peccaries, rabbits, mice, rats, and snakes. Edible desert plants such as the prickly pear, mesquite bean pods, maguey, and a variety of roots, herbs, and *guelites* (greens) supplemented the hunt. In some areas nature provided so abundantly that the inhabitants had little incentive to undertake agriculture and instead could wander freely. For example, in the coastal regions of present-day California, acorns fell so profusely from the trees that the Indians could gather them as a daily staple, along with the plentiful fruits, berries, and game animals. The Seri Indians, living in what is now the Mexican state of Sonora, caught enough fish and sea turtles in the Gulf of California to feed themselves without agriculture. The Gulf of Mexico, particularly around the Rio Grande delta, yielded a similarly rich catch, although maize agriculture had begun to make inroads in this region when the Spaniards arrived. Even some inland areas, such as the confluence of the Rio Grande and the Rio Conchos, offered plentiful freshwater mussels and fish, but again not to the exclusion of floodplain agriculture.[4]

The nomadic life of the California and Seri Indians contrasted sharply with the lifestyle in the Pueblo villages along the Rio Grande and the Little Colorado and Pecos rivers. Irrigated maize agriculture supported large communities, in some cases numbering in the thousands and living in multistory mud-brick apartment houses. The Pueblo Indians consumed the staple corn in a variety of ways: toasted, boiled, and as gruel. In addition, the Spanish conquistadors described the making of tortillas and tamales; indeed, Coronado praised the Zuni tortillas as the best he had ever eaten. Nevertheless, the Spaniards did not mention the use of chiles, the principal flavoring of central Mexico. The Pueblo people also raised domesticated turkeys, but their sedentary life and advanced agriculture did not preclude hunting and gathering. Piñon nuts, gathered in the fall, added greatly to the Pueblo diet, and the Pecos Indians even ventured out onto the Great Plains to hunt bison. The people at Pecos may also have caught large amounts of trout, while the Zuni considered fish taboo.[5]

The majority of the Southwestern Indians were semi-sedentary, growing maize while still depending heavily on hunting and gathering. Called *rancheria* people by the Spaniards, they generally lived in bands numbering two to three hundred, spread out over considerable distances, and often migrating during the course of the year. The rancheria people comprised the Tarahumara and Conchos of the western Sierra Madre (Chihuahua); the Yaqui and Mayo, inhabiting river valleys of the same names; as well as their northern neighbors, the Lower Pima and Opata (Sonora), the Yuma in the Colorado River valley, and the Upper Pima and Tohono O'odham along various rivers in the Sonoran Desert (northwestern Sonora and southern Arizona). In addition, the Athabaskan-speaking people later known as Navajos and Apaches had recently migrated into the region from the north and were beginning to cultivate maize when the Spaniards arrived. While much of their harvest of corn, beans, and squash was simply roasted along with any game they may have caught, the rancheria people made *pinole* by adding toasted and ground maize seeds to water, and baked loaves of corn and mesquite bread. Some also drank a mildly alcoholic beverage of fermented cactus fruit.[6]

A common theme unified the lives of these otherwise disparate peoples, that of constant movement. Even the most settled Puebloans had to relocate regularly, rebuilding their adobe homes in the process, in order to find more fertile land in the arid climate. The agricultural Pueblo societies were matrilineal, and some authors have suggested that women may have fared better there than in the patriarchal hunter-gatherer societies of California. Moreover, the Pueblo Indians worshipped Corn Mothers as fertility symbols at the heart of their religious beliefs, while the rancheria peoples, who had adopted agriculture more recently, attached less religious significance to corn. But regardless whether the Native Americans believed in animal spirits or corn goddesses, their encounter with Spanish priests changed their diet as well as their religion.[7]

FRONTIER FOODS OF NEW SPAIN

The conquistadors' mission of Europeanizing the Americas—literally founding a New Spain—required the simultaneous introduction of Old World plants and animals and the extirpation of native foods associated with heathen religious practices. Father Bernardino de Sahagin instructed the Indians to eat "that which the Castilian people eat, because it is good food, that with which they are raised, they are strong and pure and wise . . . You will become the same way if you eat their food."[8] Yet his nutritional advice, like much of the Catholic doctrine, was accepted only halfway. Native Americans embraced some new foods, particularly livestock, while clinging stubbornly to their staple crops of maize, beans, squash, and chiles. A mestizo cuisine eventually emerged, combining foods from the Old World and the New, just as intermarriage between Spaniards and Indians produced Mexico's mestizo nation. These mixtures spread to the northern provinces as well, and on that distant frontier, mestizo society and culture were often mistaken for Spanish originals.

Catholic priests, whose evangelical mission to the Indians served to justify Spain's empire in the Americas, demanded radical changes in the lives of the new initiates. The European belief that civilization required permanent settlements brought an end to the nomadic or semi-nomadic lifestyle of many rancheria peoples, although the introduction of livestock compensated in part for the decline in hunting. Prohibitions on polygamy, together with the introduction of European diseases against which the natives had little resistance, decimated the indigenous social organization. Natives responded to these changes in different ways; the Yaquis embraced the missions, adopting far more of the newly emerging Mexican culture, including the cooking techniques, than did the neighboring Mayo. Among the Athabaskan people, some settled down to become sheepherders, blending their culture with that of the Pueblos and taking the name Navajo. Others took only the Spanish horses, and by the 1660s, the Apaches, as they were called, had become a menace to both Spanish and Pueblo settlements. Pacification policies encouraged further acculturation through handouts of food and alcohol to make the Apaches dependent on Spanish officials and the distribution of defective firearms to limit the destruction when they did go on raids.[9]

If the spiritual conquest legitimized the colonies, the prospect of making a quick fortune attracted Spanish settlers. After looting the Aztec Empire, the conquistadors set out for the north in search of the fabled Seven Cities of Cibola, where legend had it that the streets were paved with gold. The expedition of Francisco Vásquez de Coronado reached the Zuni Pueblos in 1540, discovering the reality to be a more prosaic adobe. The silver bonanza at Zacarecas in 1548 attracted the first permanent European settlement in the north and also led to the construction of presidios to protect the treasure on the Royal Road back to Mexico City. Juan de Oñate, a silver miner made wealthy in Zacarecas, established the colony of New Mexico in 1598, although the Pueblo Revolt of 1680 temporarily forced the Spaniards to withdraw to El Paso del Norte. The rest of the Southwest remained unsettled by Europeans until the eighteenth century, when imperial defense requirements promoted a more active Spanish presence. French incursions from Louisiana into Texas led to the foundation of San Antonio in 1718, while Apache raids in Sonora motivated the construction of a presidio at Tucson in 1776. Finally, the appearance of Russian trappers on the northern Pacific coast prompted the crown to transfer troops from Sonora and Sinaloa to new presidios in California.[10]

The new settlers, although generally mestizos from central Mexico, attempted to construct a Spanish society on the northern frontier. The Iberian Peninsula had a medieval tradition of mounted cattle raising—the vaquero culture later appropriated by Anglo cowboys—but the scrawny range cattle were often butchered for their hides alone, leaving the meat behind to rot. The settlers preferred sheep and goats, especially prizing *cabrito asado* (roast kid) as a delicacy throughout the frontier region. Cooking techniques often amounted to methods of preservation such as making cheese or sausage. The colonists also produced large amounts of *carne seca*, a form of jerky made by cutting beef into long strips and drying it in the desert sun inside a cage to keep the flies out. To preserve pork, they made a vinegar marinade called *adovo*, heavily spiced with chiles to distinguish it from similar Spanish preparations. Whenever irrigation permitted, the settlers cultivated the European grain wheat, although the expense of mills and ovens often forced women to grind the grain on metates and cook it in the form of tortillas rather than bread. The pervasive use of chiles in stews and salsas likewise demonstrated the Native American influence on Spanish cuisine. The rich agricultural land of California allowed the production of those Mediterranean staples, wine and olives, unavailable elsewhere in New Spain, but even the wealthiest settlers ate a generally Spartan diet with only an occasional luxury such as imported chocolate. Those sturdy frontier foods later became the foundation for Southwestern cuisine and a bulwark of Mexican American identity.[11]

DECONSTRUCTING CHILI/E

Chili or chile? Chili con carne or carne con chile? Chile verde or carne verde? Southwestern cuisine often seems as baffling as it is intimidating to newcomers who have not yet developed a tolerance for spicy foods. The confusion derives from both regional and temporal differences; for example, a person who asks, "Red or green?" is now answering the question, "Where are you? New Mexico." Prior to refrigeration, the color question was seasonal, had the fresh green chiles ripened and turned red while drying on the *ristra*? But however varied their cooking styles, Hispanics in the Southwest faced a common question that struck to the heart of their identity: were they Mexican or Spanish? For more than a century after the United States annexed the region, former Mexican citizens, accustomed to fluid racial boundaries, struggled to find a place in a society that saw only black and white. They claimed Spanish descent in an attempt to gain equal status as Europeans, but in doing so, often shunned their fellow Mexicans who had migrated north more recently. The permutations of chile reflect the diverse experiences of Hispanics as they encountered Anglo society and established their citizenship in the United States.[12]

New Mexico, the oldest European settlement in North America, also has the most firmly established cuisine in the Southwest. Centered around the capital, Santa Fe, this cooking style extends beyond the geographical confines of the state to include the San Luis Valley in southern Colorado, the mountains around Flagstaff in northern Arizona, and parts of Chihuahua, Mexico. The soul of Mexican cuisine has always been the chile pepper, but while the cooks of Old Mexico experimented with blending different chiles to make their renowned *mole* sauces, in New Mexico they perfected the cultivation and cooking of a single chile. The state's eponymous pepper forms the basic ingredient for both chile verde and chile colorado, which can be served thick as a sauce or with broth and vegetables as a stew, although in the latter case the green is more common, sometimes with the name carne con chile verde or chile verde *caldo* to distinguish it from the sauce. For those unable to choose between the two sauces, restaurants in New Mexico offer a combination of red and green known as Christmas. Unlike Mexican moles, which gain their taste and texture from freshly ground peppers, chile colorado is often simply a mixture of chile powder and water, perhaps thickened by a roux, with garlic, oregano, and salt to taste. As Santa Fe cooking authority Huntley Dent explains, red chile "savors of mystique, not so much for its own taste, which is earthy and fairly musty, as for its ability to combine with corn tortillas, meat, and cheese."[13]

The traditional cooking of New Mexico comprises a variety of dishes, often made with distinctive local twists. The celebrated blue corn and the little-known *chicos* (roasted green ears) are both hallmarks of the state, which is also the only place cooks serve the hominy dish *posole* as a vegetable side order rather than a meaty stew. Pork rather than beef came to replace kid and mutton as the most common meat, used both for chile stews and the colonial dish *carne adovada*, which remains a favorite in New Mexico. Meals end with such distinctive desserts as the fried-bread *sopaipillas* and *buñuelos* or the enigmatic sprouted-wheat pudding *panocha*. Moreover, different cooking styles appear within New Mexico, particularly in the rivalry between north and south. The residents of Chimayó and Española take pride in the intense flavor their diminutive chiles develop while shivering in the shadows of the Sangre de Cristo Mountains. "Down there in the south," explained farmer Orlando Casados Sr., "a lot of those chiles are as big as a banana, but they taste like cardboard, no flavor at all. This is the best place for growing chile in the whole world." Nevertheless, people down south in the "Chile Capital" of Hatch, New Mexico, feel equally proud of the *rellenus* (stuffed chiles) served at their annual Chile Festival. Hispanics in Colorado meanwhile consider their chile verde superior because of the quality of the local pork.[14]

The regional cooking of Sonora, encompassing both the Mexican state and the southern half of Arizona, gave much less emphasis to the heat of the chile pepper. The classic New Mexico stew carne con chile verde changed so radically when made with mild Anaheim peppers that some Arizona cooks dropped the word "chile" entirely and referred to it simply as "carne verde." The dish also featured beef instead of pork, a tribute to the herds of cattle raised in the valleys of the Sonoran Desert. Even after the advent of refrigeration, one of the most common methods of preparing beef remained the colonial style of jerky, sometimes called *machaca*, for the pounding needed to reconstitute it. Cookbook author Diana Kennedy noted that cooks throughout the state of Sonora kept a large black pebble for this purpose. Flour tortillas, while common throughout the Southwest, also reached the peak of artistry in Sonora, where cooks often roll them out to perfectly round, paper-thin disks a foot and a half in diameter. When wrapped around beef or bean fillings to make burritos, they became "possibly the single heaviest fast-food item in the world," which in turn took the name *chimichanga* (basically meaning "thing-amajig") when deep fried.[15]

New Mexico and Arizona shared a common isolation, which kept the territories from reaching full statehood in the nineteenth century and also allowed the Mexican communities to retain their cultural integrity. Of course, Anglos came to dominate politics and most Hispanics remained strictly working class; nevertheless, a substantial Mexican American middle class preserved its economic position and cultural heritage by renaming it Spanish. Eventually, the same rugged mountains and stark desert landscapes that had repelled immigrants in the nineteenth century attracted them when air conditioning and ski lifts arrived following World War II, leading to a real estate boom that drove increasing numbers of Hispanics from their land around Santa Fe, Taos, and Tucson. By contrast, Mexicans in Texas and California did not have a century of isolation to consolidate their social position, for the dispossession of land followed immediately on the Treaty of Guadalupe Hidalgo.[16]

While the origins of Texas's chile con carne remain shrouded in culinary legend, the subsequent development of the dish reveals a process of both racial stereotyping and cultural appropriation. The dish probably began as a stew, made of goat or deer meat as often as beef, and spiced with red chiles, cumin, and oregano, which remain the distinctive flavors of Tex-Mex cooking as cooking expert Marilyn Tausend has observed. Subtleties of taste were lost on Anglo visitors to nineteenth-century San Antonio, who rarely made it past the initial shock of the chile peppers. In 1874, for example, Edward King described "fat, swarthy Mexican mater-familias" offering "various savory compounds, swimming in fiery pepper, which biteth like a serpent." The imagined dangers, both culinary and sexual, of the so-called chili queens on Military Plaza enticed countless tourists, who remembered the city "because of the Chili Stands, the Menger Hotel, and the Alamo." But the Hispanic cooks did not share in the profits from mass-marketing their dish; in 1896, a German immigrant, William Gebhardt, formulated the chili powder known as Tampico Dust, which helped spread the taste for chili across the country. Already tamed down for timid palates, chili underwent other alterations, the side order of beans was unceremoniously dumped into the pot, and it was added to hot dogs and, in Cincinnati, even to spaghetti. Meanwhile, back in San Antonio, after a long struggle with city inspectors, the original chili stands closed down as supposed health hazards in the 1930s.[17]

Chili had been stripped of its ethnicity to become the state dish of Texas, but Mexican Americans retained a repertoire of other foods that affirmed their identity precisely because of the scorn they attracted from the Anglo elite. Although it had lost favor in New Mexico and California, cabrito asado remained as popular in south Texas as in northeastern Mexico, particularly Monterrey, where it attained legendary status. Anglos had little use for goat, but the only beef that poor Mexican Americans could afford was the viscera. One such castoff cut, the diaphragm muscle (*arrachera*), lost its tough texture in a marinade of lime juice and garlic and became quite delicious when grilled on an open fire and served with salsa on hot, fresh tortillas. Perhaps the most beloved dish of working-class Mexican Americans, and the most repulsive one to outsiders, was the pit-barbecued bull head (*barbacoa de cabeza*). The two-day process of preparing the pit, cooking the meat, and serving it up messily as tacos invited communal celebrations, drinking, and dancing among Hispanics.[18]

Legends of Texas chili notwithstanding, the most mysterious branch of Southwestern cuisine is the original art of California ranch cooking. Unlike the thriving Hispanic cultures of New Mexico, Arizona, and south Texas, Californio society now exists only as a memory, distorted by the assimilation of a small elite into Anglo society and by more recent Mexican migrants, who far outnumber the descendants of the original settlers. Nevertheless, a few tastes of that pastoral era can be gleaned from the first Spanish-language cookbook published in the state, *El cocinero español* (1898) by Encarnación Pinedo. An heiress to one of the most prominent Californio families, the Berreyesa clan, she was born in the tragic year of 1848, as a swarm of Anglo fortune hunters descended to swindle away the family estates and to lynch eight of her uncles and cousins. Determined to maintain the dignity of Hispanic culture, Pinedo gave a stinging rebuke to the barbarous Yankee invaders, describing their food as "the most insipid and tasteless that one can imagine." Her own recipes, written in a lively literary style, derived from classical Mexican dishes such as moles, tamales, chiles rellenos, and barbacoa de cabeza, even though she disguised them with Spanish titles. As Victor Valle has observed, "The Mexican roots of [modern] California cuisine can also be detected in her liberal use of fruits and vegetables, fresh edible flowers and herbs, her aggressive spicing, and grilling over native wood fires."[19]

Pinedo's cookbook provided an eloquent example of Hispanics' widespread use of food to affirm their identity against the threat of Anglo encroachment. Jacqueline Higuera McMahan has written a series of nostalgic cookbooks, laden with family history, which describe the culinary encounters of old California. The Yankee newcomers were apparently so astonished to see people eat chiles for breakfast that they attributed to Californios the digestive system of ostriches. The Higueras meanwhile repeated the fiction that they had lost their Santa Clara ranch to finance the legendary 1865 wedding festival of Don Valentin's favorite daughter, Maria. Although declining in society, the family at least took comfort from the belief that they had a more civilized lifestyle than the Anglo land grabbers around them. Twentieth-century migrants brought their own regional dishes with them from Mexico and often used these foods to defend themselves against racial discrimination. Victor Villaseñor, in his best-selling family memoir, *Rain of Gold*, recalled his grandmother's words, "Don't worry about the police. One day we'll feed them tacos with so much old chile that they'll get diarrhea and their assholes will burn for weeks!"[20]

Encounters between ethnic foods and mainstream consumers have remained sites of cultural contention throughout the twentieth century, as Mexicans faced the contradictory impulses to preserve their culture intact or to profit from adapting the foods for a general audience. Enclave restaurants sprang up wherever large numbers of Mexicans settled more or less permanently to work. By the beginning of the century, such small-time establishments existed all along the border as well as in more distant urban areas such as Chicago, St. Louis, and Kansas City. Moreover, many restaurants acquired a Mexican character when Anglo owners discovered the profits they could make by allowing their Hispanic kitchen staff to cook their own foods. One such successful restaurateur, who had started out with just a shack selling hamburgers and barbecue in Tucson and was facing ruin when his Mexican cook quit, begged her to write down the formulas. "Oh, no," Esperanza Montoya Padilla replied, "I'm dumb enough to work for you, but I'm not dumb enough to give you my recipes!"[21]

The combination plate, rarely seen in Mexico but one of the mainstays of Mexican American restaurants, may have originated in Texas early in the twentieth century as an adaptation to Anglo customers. Tacos, enchiladas, tostadas, and burritos, known collectively as *antojitos* (little whimsies), had long provided quick meals to working-class Mexicans, who often ate them standing on a street corner. Mainstream diners required a more formal meal, including a plate and silverware, so Hispanic cooks complied, perhaps spreading quantities of red chili sauce on top because the customers were using forks anyway. Anglo expectations for a quick plate full of food, as opposed to the Mexican preference for separate, smaller courses, encouraged cooks to combine the main dish with rice (usually eaten prior to the main course) and beans (eaten after). Numbering the combination plates relieved non-Spanish speakers of the need to pronounce what they were eating, a strategy also adopted by Chinese cooks seeking a crossover clientele. About 1940, the combination plate even made its way back to Mexico when flamboyant restaurateur José Inés Loredo created his signature dish, *carne asada a la tampiqueña*. This butterflied and grilled filet, served with poblano chile strips, two green enchiladas, a bowl of frijoles, and a piece of grilled cheese, introduced the regional foods of Loredo's hometown, Tampico, to residents of Mexico City.[22]

Small restaurants have a high mortality rate, and Mexican American establishments are no exception; nevertheless a few have survived through the years to attain the status of enduring monuments. The names of these restaurants have become local legends: in Los Angeles, El Cholo, founded in 1923 as the Sonora Café; Tucson's El Charro Café, dating back to 1922; La Posta, which opened in Mesilla, New Mexico, in 1939; and Mi Tierra, located on San Antonio's Market Square since 1951. Outstanding kitchens provided the common foundation for these culinary monuments, but their fame spread far beyond their ethnic enclave in part because of celebrity endorsements. El Cholo became a watering hole for Hollywood stars from Clark Cable and Bing Crosby to Jack Nicholson and Madonna. Western movies filmed on location near Tucson in the 1940s gave El Charro an opportunity to bask in Hollywood publicity. More recently, national attention focused on Mi Tierra when a photojournalist caught President Bill Clinton wearing one of their T-shirts while jogging on a beach.[23]

Countless restaurants have sought to lure non-Mexican customers through identification with celebrities, either by decorating their walls with autographed photos or by affixing small plaques to the tables. Such endorsements offered a cheap substitute for advertising in order to build up a brand name as well as a surrogate form of authenticity in a multi-ethnic marketplace. This familiarity may have been particularly valuable when mainstream eaters lacked sufficient knowledge of an ethnic cuisine to distinguish quality food from bowdlerized imitations. A similar purpose was served by culinary legends, endlessly repeated, about which Southwestern restaurateur named Ignacio invented nachos, or who created the original margarita, or the first green enchiladas with chicken and sour cream. These tales often reveal a desire for acceptance of ethnic foods by the broader society; for example, the owners of El Charro Café recall a visit, in 1946, by Thomas E. Dewey in which the presidential candidate supposedly mistook one of the soft, thin flour tortillas for a napkin and tucked it into his collar. The Dewey Napkin exhibited the same characteristics as the legendary origins of Mexican mole, created by colonial nuns out of a mixture of Old World spices and New World chiles—just like the mestizo nation—and served up for the approval of the Spanish viceroy. In the Southwest, these urban legends gently chide Anglos for their unfamiliarity with Mexican food and by extension their society. Perhaps the most famous tells of President Gerald Ford eating a tamale without taking off the husk.[24]

Another route to financial success for Mexican American restaurants in the postwar era came from the development of franchise chains. The largest of these, El Chico, began in 1931 with Adelaida "Mama" Cuellar's tamale stand at the Kaufman County Fair. After losing a number of small-town cafes in the depression, the family moved to Dallas and opened the first El Chico in 1940. When the war ended, the Cuellar brothers began expanding, locally at first and eventually throughout the South and Southwest, before selling the restaurants in the 1990s. Another chain based in the Dallas–Fort Worth area, Pulidos, began in the 1950s with an immigrant family from Zacarecas. The Pulidos weathered economic downturns by self-financing new locations, often taking over defunct restaurants, and by expanding into small towns where they faced little competition. Although the menu catered predominantly to Anglo customers, the tamales remained an authentic Mexican taste because they were made by hand every morning by Mrs. Pulido and her two comadres.[25]

Despite the success of culinary monuments and Southwestern chains, Mexican American food did not attain a national presence until it was taken over by non-Mexican corporations such as Taco Bell. Sociologist George Ritzer has described the spread of fast-food restaurants—"McDonaldization" he calls it—as the continuation of Max Weber's rationalization process whereby technology imposes greater efficiency, predictability, and control on society.[26] This explanation certainly applies to the restaurant chain founded in 1962 by Glen Bell in Downey, California. Rather than compete for the hamburger market with Ray Kroc, in nearby San Bernardino, Bell devised a way to speed up the production of tacos by pre-frying the corn tortillas, thus creating the prototype for the hard taco shell. Mexican-style food was thereby released from the need for fresh tortillas, allowing the chain to expand throughout the country. The corporation went public in 1969, was bought by Pepsi-Co. in 1978, and then spun off in Tricon Global Restaurants with Pizza Hut and KFC in 1997. With more than 4,600 locations worldwide, and with look-alike competitors such as Del Taco, Taco Time, and Taco Tico, Taco Bell defined Mexican food for an entire generation in the United States. The mass-market appropriation of Mexican food, which began with Tampico Dust and racial slurs about chili queens, thus culminated in chants of "Viva Gorditas!" by the Taco Bell dog. Nevertheless, as tourism and migration gave consumers a greater awareness of genuine Mexican cuisine, a culinary renaissance became possible.

THE BLUE CORN BONANZA

Taco Bell had skimmed the surface, or perhaps dredged the bottom, of Mexican American foods, but a wealth of Southwestern dishes awaited discovery by consumers. Santa Fe finally grabbed the nation's gastronomic imagination in the 1980s, after a lengthy search for authentic regional cuisines from the United States that could compete with those of France, Italy, and China. Once the trend began, Southwestern food quickly became so common that, in 1987, M. F. K. Fisher groaned, "If I hear any more about chic Tex-Mex or blue cornmeal, I'll throw up." Nevertheless, her complaints went unheeded, as corporate versions of Mexican food filled supermarkets across the country. That this was not just a temporary fad became clear in 1991, when salsa surpassed catsup as the best-selling condiment in the United States. This rapid success did nothing to diminish but rather heightened the tension between authenticity and adaptation that had so long bedeviled Southwestern cooking.[27]

The birth of a modern, upscale restaurant version of traditional Southwestern cooking had a long gestation period—most notably in the cookbooks, newspaper columns, and ecological awareness of James Beard, Craig Claiborne, and Alice Waters—so that when it finally emerged, it soon became ubiquitous. John Rivera Sedlar, a native of New Mexico who pioneered this new style in 1980, recalled, "When I first began serving tortillas, tamales, and chiles in a fine-dining environment, people gasped." Shortly thereafter, Robert Del Grande in Houston and Stephan Pyles in Dallas did for Texas cooking what Sedlar had done for New Mexico. In 1987, Mark Miller, a former anthropology student with a deep knowledge of the foods and cultures of Latin America, opened the acclaimed Coyote Café in Santa Fe. Where ethnic restaurants had earlier pursued celebrities as advertisements, the chefs suddenly found themselves to be celebrities—for example, television's "Too Hot Tamales," Mary Sue Milliken and Susan Feniger. As the field grew increasingly crowded, Jay McCarthy sought recognition by proclaiming himself the "Cactus King," followed by Lenard Rubin, the "Cilantro King." Of course, much of this nouvelle Southwestern cuisine bore only a superficial resemblance to either Mexican or Mexican American cooking; witness Pyles's signature dish, a seared foie gras corn pudding tamale with pineapple mole and canela dust. Nevertheless, similar concoctions began to appear in some of the most expensive restaurants in Mexico City.[28]

Supermarket sales of tortillas, chips, salsas, and other Mexican foods meanwhile grew into a three-billion-dollar market by the mid-1990s, although only a small fraction of this revenue went to Hispanic-owned businesses. Indeed, the industry has been dominated by Anglos since Elmer Doolin purchased the formula for Fritos corn chips from a nameless Mexican American in 1932 and Dave Pace began bottling salsa in 1948. Just three corporations controlled more than half the nation's salsa market: Pace, owned by Campbell Soup Co.; Tostitos, a brand of Frito-Lay; and Old El Paso, a subsidiary of Pillsbury. Boutique producers meanwhile contended for a more upscale niche with outlandish claims of authenticity. Fire Roasted Zuni Zalsa attributed its origins to a mythical Mexican past: "The old patron walked down the mountainside overlooking the jalapeño field. He paused, turned to young Josélita [sic] and said, 'Make me a salsa, make me a salsa I can't refuse.'" Local Mexican American manufacturers did better with corn tortillas because of their brief shelf life, but the bulk of sales in the United States went for flour tortillas, often stripped of their original ethnic character by cinnamon or pesto flavoring and marketed as "wraps."[29]

Yet the search for authenticity, or at least for product differentiation, led back again and again to Mexico. The quintessential dish of modern Tex-Mex, fajitas, started out as the vaquero's humble arrachera, served up on a fancy grill but eaten in the style of all Mexican tacos, with salsa on hot and, one hopes, fresh tortillas. In the 1980s, the fad drove the price of skirt steak out of the reach of the working-class Hispanics who invented the dish and also led to that oxymoron "chicken fajitas." One of the hottest items of the 1990s, the fish taco, was discovered by surfers such as Ralph Rubio while vacationing in Baja, California, and became part of the new Cal-Mex cuisine, especially around San Diego. At the same time, growing numbers of Tex-Mex restaurants in New York City have begun to replace burritos and fajitas with regional Mexican dishes from Oaxaca and Veracruz, dumping the serapes and mariachi music in the process. Even in the Dallas–Fort Worth area, restaurateur Chris Aparicio reported optimistically, "You used to have to have Tex-Mex food to survive. We serve authentic Mexican and our clientele used to be 80 percent Hispanic. Now it's 60 percent Anglo and 40 percent Hispanic. People are catching on to the true flavor of Mexican food."[30]

The real question about the blue corn bonanza remains, who will benefit from it? Mexicans dreamed of finding the legendary Seven Cities of Cibola for three centuries, only to lose their northern provinces in 1848, a year before gold was finally discovered in California. As Victor Valle has explained, too few of the Anglo owners of Mexican restaurants and food-processing companies are willing to give anything back to the communities that made their fortunes, even by paying decent wages and offering equal employment opportunities. But Valle also strikes a more positive note, pointing to the Mexican immigrants and Mexican Americans who have begun to reclaim their foods in upscale restaurants around the country as well as in factories turning out authentic foodstuffs. Joe Sánchez of the New El Rey Chorizo Company did not feel threatened by large corporate competitors. "So we are not going to disappear. We'll progress. And the big chain stores will have to stock two sections of Mexican food; the tourist food for the Anglos and the real Mexican food for the Mexicans. And then, since many Anglos like real Mexican food, they'll go over to the Mexican section and buy real ingredients, too."[31]

CONCLUSION: WHOSE MEX?

Douglas Monroy titled his study of early California society, "Thrown among Strangers," evoking the similar experiences of Native Americans forced to work on Spanish missions and Hispanic ranchers displaced by Anglo capitalists. For much the same reason, an account of the foods of the Southwest could easily be called "Fed to Foreigners." Native American women of the pueblos cooked tortillas for the Spanish conquistadors, only to have their corn mother deities denounced by Catholic priests in return. Hispanic women in San Antonio served up chili stews to Anglo tourists three hundred years later, losing their businesses to industrial mass producers and city health inspectors in the process. Even their erstwhile compatriots abandoned the Mexican Americans, denouncing chili con carne as a "detestable food with false Mexican title that is sold in the United States of the North," in the words of linguist Francisco J. Santamaria.[32]

Despite calumny from all sides, Tejanas continue to treasure their "bowls of red" as a hearty, restorative food, made by hand according to old family recipes and served with pride to friends and relatives. Carne con chile verde holds an equally revered status in the kitchens of New Mexico, as do burritos de carne seca in Arizona and tacos de carnitas in California. Even if only once a year at a holiday tamalada, Mexican Americans reaffirm their connections to family and community, the past and the future, through the ritual preparation and consumption of traditional foods. Neither commercialization, mass production, McDonaldization, Yuppification, nor any other menace of modern life has alienated these foods from cooks, both Hispanic and non-Hispanic, who invest the time to prepare them. The "Mex" thus belongs to anyone willing to embrace it.

NOTES

1. For a history of Mexican cuisine, see Jeffrey M. Pilcher, ¡Que Vivan Los Tamales! Food and the Making of Mexican Identity (Albuquerque: University of New Mexico Press, 1998).

2. The Border Cookbook: Authentic Home Cooking of the American Southwest and Northern Mexico (Boston: The Harvard Common Press, 1995).

3. Victor Valle argues persuasively for the culinary metaphor of the mixed-race mestizo in his scholarly and mouthwatering cookbook, Recipes of Memory: Five Generations of Mexican Cuisine in Los Angeles (New York: The New Press, 1995), 175–77. Another insightful treatment is Amy Bently, "From Culinary Other to Mainstream American: Meanings and Uses of Southwestern Cuisine," Southern Folkore 55, no. 3 (1998): 238–52. On the gendered nature of the frontier, see Fredrick Pike, The United States and Latin America: Myths and Stereotypes of Civilization and Nature (Austin: University of Texas Press, 1992); and more generally Edward W. Said, Orientalism (New York: Random House, 1979).

4. Douglas Monroy, Thrown among Strangers: The Making of Mexican Culture in Frontier California (Berkeley: University of California Press, 1990), 3–18; Edward H. Spicer, Cycles of Conquest: The Impact of Spain, Mexico, and the United States on the Indians of the Southwest, 1533–1960 (Tucson: University of Arizona Press, 1962), 14–15; Martin Salinas, Indians of the Rio Grande Delta: Their Role in the History of Southern Texas and Northeastern Mexico (Austin: University of Texas Press, 1990), 115–20; Carroll L. Riley, The Frontier People: The Greater Southwest in the Protohistoric Period (Albuquerque: University of New Mexico Press, 1987), 298–300.

5. Riley, Frontier People, 184–87, 232–34, 260–63.

6. Ibid., 114–16, 142; Spicer, Cycles of Conquest, 12–14, 541.

7. Ramon A. Gurierrez, When Jesus Came, the Corn Mothers Went Away (Stanford: Stanford University Press, 1991), 14–16; Monroy, Thrown among Strangers, 8–9; Spicer, Cycles of Conquest, 541.

8. Louise M. Burkhart, The Slippery Earth: Nahua-Christian Moral Dialogue in Sixteenth-Century Mexico (Tucson: University of Arizona Press, 1989), 166.

9. David J. Weber, The Spanish Frontier in North America (New Haven: Yale University Press, 1992), 92–121, 227–30; Cynthia Radding, Wandering Peoples: Colonialism, Ethnic Spaces, and Ecological Frontiers in Northwestern Mexico, 1700–1850 (Durham: Duke University Press, 1997), 48–60; Spicer, Cycles of Conquest, 542–46, 552; Albert H. Schroeder, "Shifting for Survival in the Spanish Southwest," in New Spain's Far Northern Frontier: Essays on Spain in the American West, 1540–1821, ed. David J. Weber (Albuquerque: University of New Mexico Press, 1979), 243–44.

10. Oakah E. Jones Jr., Los Paisanos: Spanish Settlers on the Northern Frontier of New Spain (Norman: University of Oklahoma Press, 1979); Jesus F. de la Teja, San Antonio de Bexar: A Community on New Spain's Northern Frontier (Albuquerque: University of New Mexico Press, 1995); John I. Kessell, Kiva, Cross and Crown: The Pecos Indians and New Mexico, 1540–1840 (Washington, DC: National Park Service, 1979); Max L. Moorhead, The Presidio: Bastion of the Spanish Borderlands (Norman: University of Oklahoma Press, 1975).

11. Arthur L. Campa, Hispanic Culture in the Southwest (Norman: University of Oklahoma Press, 1979), 277–81; Patricia Preciado Martin, Songs My Mother Sang to Me: An Oral History of Mexican American Women (Tucson: University of Arizona Press, 1992), 11, 16, 28; Jones, Los Paisanos, 187, 194, 221.

12. Victor Valle, "A Curse of Tea and Potatoes: Reading a 19th Century Cookbook as a Social Text," Latino Studies Journal 8, no. 3 (fall 1997): 3–18. For a historical discussion that locates Hispanics within U.S. race relations, see Neil Foley, The White Scourge: Mexicans, Blacks, and Poor Whites in Texas Cotton Culture (Berkeley: University of California Press, 1997).

13. Huntley Dent, *The Feast of Santa Fe: Cooking of the American Southwest* (New York: Simon and Schuster, 1985), 73. See also Cleofas M. Jaramillo, *The Genuine New Mexico Tasty Recipes* (Santa Fe: Ancient City Press, [1942] 1981), 4; Regina Romero, *Flora's Kitchen: Recipes from a New Mexico Family* (Tucson: Treasure Chest Books, 1998), 37–46.

14. Quote from Carmella Padilla, *The Chile Chronicles: Tales of a New Mexico Harvest* (Santa Fe: Museum of New Mexico Press, 1997), 48; Fabiola Cabeza de Baca Gilbert, *The Good Life: New Mexico Traditions and Food* (Santa Fe: Museum of New Mexico Press, [1949] 1982); personal communication from Marco Antonio Abarca, January 25, 2000.

15. Quote from Merrill Shindler, *El Chola Cookbook: Recipes and Love from California's Best-Loved Mexican Kitchen* (Santa Monica: Angel City Press, 1998), 85. See also Diana Kennedy, *The Cuisines of Mexico* (New York: Harper & Row, 1986), 244; Martin, *Songs My Mother Sang to Me*, 17, 39, 155; Jay Ann Cox, "Eating the Other" (Ph.D. diss., University of Arizona, 1993).

16. For just a few examples of this voluminous literature, see Richard Griswold del Castillo, *La Familia: The Mexican American Family in the Urban Southwest* (Notre Dame: University of Notre Dame Press, 1984); idem, *The Treaty of Guadalupe Hidalgo: A Legacy of Conflict* (Norman: University of Oklahoma Press, 1990); Armando C. Alonzo, *Tejano Legacy: Rancheros and Settlers in South Texas, 1734–1900* (Albuquerque: University of New Mexico Press, 1998); Lisbeth Haas, *Conquests and Historical Identities in California, 1769–1936* (Berkeley: University of California Press, 1995); Oscar J. Martinez, *Troublesome Border* (Tucson: University of Arizona Press, 1988); Thomas E. Sheridan, *Los Tucsonenses: The Mexican Community in Tucson, 1854–1941* (Tucson: University of Arizona Press, 1986).

17. The best account of the appropriation of ethnic foods is Donna R. Gabaccia, *We Are What We Eat: Ethnic Foods and the Making of Americans* (Cambridge: Harvard University Press, 1998), quotations are from 108-9. See also Marilyn Tausend, *Cocina de la familia* (New York: Simon & Schuster, 1997), 66; Mary Ann Noonan Guerra, *The History of San Antonio's Market Square* (San Antonio: The Alamo Press, 1988), 14, 48.

18. Mario Montaño, "The History of Mexican Folk Foodways of South Texas Street Vendors, Offal Foods, and Barbacoa de Cabeza" (Ph.D. diss., University of Pennsylvania, 1992); José E. Eamón, *Dancing with the Devil: Society and Cultural Poetics in Mexican American South Texas* (Madison: University of Wisconsin Press, 1994).

19. Valle, "A Curse of Tea and Potatoes," quoted from 9, 12. The Pinedo volume has been edited and translated by Dan Strelil as *The Spanish Cook: A Selection of Recipes from Encarnación Pinedo's El cocinero español* (Pasadena: The Weather Bird Press, 1992).

20. Victor Villaseñor, *Rain of Gold* (New York: Delta, 1991), 350. See also Jacqueline Higuera McMahan, *The Mexican Breakfast Cookbook* (Lake Hughes, CA: The Olive Press, 1992), 116; *California Rancho Cooking* (Lake Hughes, CA: The Olive Press, 1988), 130–34.

21. Quoted in Martin, *Songs My Mother Sang to Me*, 116.

22. Jamison and Jamison, *The Border Cookbook*, 10–11.

23. Shindler, *El Cholo Cookbook*, 15; Flores, *El Charro Café* (Tucson: Fisher Books, 1998), 3.

24. This discussion was inspired by Tracy Poe, "Food Culture and Entrepreneurship among African Americans, Italians, and Swedes in Chicago" (Ph.D. diss., Harvard University, 1999). See also Flores, *El Charro Café*, 24.

25. Jeffrey Steele, "Mexican Goes Mainstream," *Restaurante Mexicano* 1, no. 1 (January/February 1997): 6–15; interview with Edward Gámez, chairman of the board of Pulido's Restaurants, Fort Worth, Texas, March 26, 1992.

26. George Ritzer, *The McDonaldization of Society* (Thousand Oaks, CA: Pine Forge Press, 1993). See also Warren J. Belasco, "Ethnic Fast Foods: The Corporate Melting Pot," *Food and Foodways* 2 (1987): 1–30.

27. Quote from Sylvia Lovegren, *Fashionable Food: Seven Decades of Food Fads* (New York: Macmillan, 1995), 378.

28. Quote from Barbara Pool Fenzl, *Savor the Southwest* (San Francisco: Bay Books, 1999), 14. See also Mark Miller, *Coyote Café* (San Francisco: Ten Speed Press, 1989); Mark Miller, Stephan Pyles, and John Sedlar, *Tamales* (New York: Macmillan, 1997); Mary Sue Milliken and Susan Feniger, *Mesa Mexicana* (New York: William Morrow, 1994).

29. Gabaccia, *We Are What We Eat*, 165, 219; "Another Round," *Snack World* 53, no. 6 (June 1996): 32; Margaret Littman, "Wrap Up Profits with Tortillas," *Bakery Production and Marketing* 31, no. 16 (November 15, 1996): 40.

30. Mario Montaño, "Appropriation and Counterhegemony in South Texas: Food Slurs, Offal Meats, and Blood," in *Usable Pasts: Traditions and Group Expressions in North America*, ed. Tad Tuleja (Logan: Utah State University Press, 1997), 50–67. Quoted in Julia M. Gallo-Torres, "Salud," *El Restaurante Mexicano* 3, no. 3 (May–June 1999): 14. See also Jane and Michael Stern, "Grill of His Dreams," *Gourmet*, January 2000, p. 40; Eric Asimov, "Beyond Tacos: Mexican Food Gets Real," *New York Times*, January 26, 2000, p. B14.

31. Valle made this point eloquently in a presentation at the Culinary Institute of America's Flavors of Mexico Conference, St. Helena, Calif., November 11, 1999, and in his book, *Recipes of Memory*, quotation on 175.

32. *Diccionario de Mejicanismos*, 5th ed. (Mexico City: Editorial Porrúa, 1992), 385.

THE TEX-MEX MENU

Helen Simons

The first European to enjoy Texas hospitality was Cabeza de Vaca, who landed on the coast of Texas in 1528. There he was served a breakfast of fish and roots by his hosts and rescuers, the Karankawa Indians. The coastal Indians in whose company he later began his journey into the unknown interior were hunters and gatherers, and among the foods they favored were mesquite beans and prickly pear. At times during his eight years and thousands of miles of wandering he went hungry because no food was available and at other times he went hungry because he found the unfamiliar foods unpalatable.

While Cabeza de Vaca was dining sparingly among the Indians of Texas and northern Mexico, the menu in other parts of the New World at the same period was much more sophisticated. A Franciscan friar, Bernardino de Sahagún, recorded Aztec life in great detail, including foodways. His sixteenth-century account, *General History of the Things of New Spain*, shows that most of the variations of Mexican food today are descendants of Aztec recipes, in which corn and chiles in several variations were basic foods. The *tlaxcalli*, a flat corn bread that was a staple of the Aztec diet, was being called *tortilla* (the Spanish word for omelet) by the 1570s and is still known by that name more than four centuries later.

In addition to corn, the New World contributed many other important foods to the Old World and, eventually, back to European settlements in North America. Peppers (including the familiar jalapeño), potatoes, tomatoes, beans, pumpkins and other squashes, sweet potatoes, peanuts, pineapples, and avocadoes as well as chocolate and vanilla, are among the many "discovered" foods that we eat or cook with today. The complete list of New World foods is much longer, but these are the most important. And of these, the most important to North American Indians were corn, squash, and beans.

Beans and squash were the earliest foods to be cultivated by Native Americans, about six or seven thousand years ago. Chiles were then brought into the garden, and in a few thousand years wild corn was tamed. Gradually over thousands of years these food plants dispersed from the agricultural centers in the south to North America. During the time known to archeologists as the Late Prehistoric, which began in Texas about 1,000 years before the arrival of the Spanish, agriculture was being practiced by village-dwelling Indians in northeast Texas, the northern Panhandle, and along the Rio Grande. Village life and the cultivation of crops brought new tools and new lifeways to these Texas Indians, but some very ancient tools, the *mano* and *metate* (a hand-held grinding stone and grinding basin or slab, used somewhat like a mortar and pestle) were found to be very useful in processing domesticated plant foods. The Mexican and Indian inhabitants of Texas were still grinding corn by the mano and metate method well into historic times.

Cabeza de Vaca, in his long trek through Texas and northern Mexico, finally encountered the farmers along the Rio Grande, who offered him squash and beans. They also grew corn, but drought had destroyed their plantings. They said that the real corn country lay to the north and west—in the land of the pueblos. Later explorers in Trans-Pecos Texas, en route to the pueblos in search of another kind of golden treasure, also encountered *rancherías* (agricultural settlements) on the Rio Grande. At La Junta de los Ríos (in the area of Presidio, Texas) the Spanish eventually established six missions, four of them on the Texas side of the river. By the mid-1700s a settlement had grown up at La Junta, and fewer than a hundred families formed the nucleus of a community that has persisted for over two hundred years. Joe Graham, an astute observer of border folkways, has said that the merging of Spanish and Indian cultures is nowhere more apparent than in the foodways of these early Mexican pioneers. To the native Indian foods both domestic and wild—including prickly pear, chiles, corn, squash, and beans—the Spanish settlers added new sources of meat such as pigs, goats, cattle, sheep, and chickens, as well as new plant foods from other areas of Mexico. Here the traditions of northern Mexico and Texas continue to blend to this day, as they do along the entire Rio Grande border. It is this blending of traditions and cross-cultural borrowing that gave rise to the style of cooking known as Tex-Mex.

Until recently serious scholars have paid scant attention to the foodways of Mexican-Americans. As with folk arts and crafts, the focus of attention has been on Mexican, rather than Mexican-American, traditions, although there are encouraging indications that change is underway. Oral history techniques are increasingly being used to record vanishing Texas lifeways. Folklife festivals, such as the one sponsored by the Institute of Texan Cultures in San Antonio, include foods along with traditional crafts and music. These often emphasize foods prepared in Mexican-American homes, which are much more varied than those that appear on restaurant menus. The family traditions involved in the making of dishes like *tamales*, the blending of Indian and Spanish foods, the preparation of foods for special celebrations (such as *bizcochitos* and tamales at Christmas, and figurine-shaped breads for El Día de los Muertos), traditional planting practices and beliefs in rural areas—all are topics for deeper study. The foods considered here are those Tex-Mex dishes that are prepared in the homes of Texans of all ethnic backgrounds, and in numerous restaurants across the state, yet are still distinctly Spanish-Indian-Mexican in character. The popularity of these foods represents the most widespread acknowledgment and acceptance of Hispanic culture in Texas.

Before ordering from the Tex-Mex menu, the newcomer to Texas should first be aware of what this food is *not*. Despite the northern Mexico influence, it is not Mexican food. Visitors who are fond of the foods of Mexico, including the traditional Spanish dishes of the interior or the seafood specialties of the coastal regions, may find themselves, like Cabeza de Vaca, on *tierra incógnita* in Texas. Neither is Tex-Mex the same as New Mexican or Californian Mexican foods, although together these are all part of a Mexican-American system that can be distinguished from the cooking of Mexico as a Southwestern North American style. However, in comparison with Tex-Mex, the traditional foods of New Mexico rely more on fresh green chiles and refined green tomatillo sauces. Green-corn tamales, made with a filling of grated young corn, green chiles, and cheese, are a good example of the delicious foods of New Mexico. California Mexican food reflects yet another style, featuring the lavish produce of the state, especially lots of avocado, garnished with sour cream and Spanish olives.

CHILI

Chili is an appropriate dish to place first in a definition of what Tex-Mex food is, since it is distinctly Texan and is, in fact, recognized as the Official State Dish (adopted in 1977). The spelling *chili* distinguishes the dish from the pepper, spelled *chile*. The novice cook should remember this distinction, since it is possible to purchase both chili powder (which is a blended mixture of all the seasonings needed to make the dish) and chile powder (which is the ground, hot pepper ingredient in chili powder). Having mastered this simple distinction, the adventurous chef, diner, historian, or folklorist is ready to proceed with a more detailed examination of the subject.

The true beginnings of chili are obscured by time and legend. A few writers have claimed that chili in some form was probably made by the Aztecs, who cultivated its basic ingredient, the hot little pepper called chilipiquín. This assertion has been challenged by Indians of the American Southwest who are certain that chili derives from a kind of pemican, dried meat ground with wild peppers, made long before the Aztecs established their great civilization and developed tortillas. However, the first recipe for chili is said to have been given to West Texas Indians in the seventeenth century by the helpful apparition of a Spanish nun known as "the Lady in Blue." (The appearance of the Lady in Blue among the Jumano Indians of West Texas is an authentic folktale, but the chili recipe variant is definitely suspect.) Some western historians, debunking both the prehistoric and seventeenth-century accounts as myth, believe that chili is actually a mid-nineteenth-century concoction, first made on trail drives by cow-camp cooks, probably using a deviled beef mixture related to the pemican made by Indians but adding water to form a kind of stew. Other historians have asserted that chili was originally cooked up in San Antonio at least as early as the 1830s by "chili queens" who worked as laundresses during the day and sold chili, made in their washtubs, in the evenings on Military Plaza. A story also has been told that chili resulted from a visiting Englishman's failed attempt to make curry using Texas Mexican ingredients. However, those who accept only the written word in the form of a bona fide recipe assert that chili was not eaten by anybody until the 1880s, when it suddenly appeared in San Antonio. In the last analysis, the honor probably really does belong to the mid-nineteenth-century cooks of San Antonio, an honor that is recognized in the city's many fiestas, when vendors in costume once again sell chili from stands in the plazas during the evenings.

The only argument about the ingredients of chili should be the central, great debate: to add beans or not to add beans to the basic meat and seasonings mixture. The meat (preferably lean beef or venison) should be chopped or coarsely ground, but many a delicious pot of chili has been made with hamburger. The only other basic ingredients besides chili powder are water and salt, but many cooks add chopped onion, garlic, and canned tomatoes. Otherwise, if it looks like chili (red) and tastes like chili (hot), it's chili. Make your own from the many recipes that are to be found in Texas newspapers, magazines, or church-group cookbooks, and keep trying till you find the one that tastes right to you. Or buy chili mix with the instructions written on the package. Do not go to a chili cook-off in search of the best chili and take all of the fixings seriously. Some entrants in these events have been known to include old leather boots in their secret recipes!

If chili is eaten as a soup or stew, with crackers, it may arguably be called simply a Texas dish. If used as a sauce, as on enchiladas, it is an authentic Tex-Mex food. From the spicy mixture sold in the plazas of San Antonio to the chuck-wagon versions served in nineteenth-century cow camps or the Helen Corbett version served at Neiman Marcus in the twentieth century, more native and naturalized Texans probably have eaten chili than any other Tex-Mex food. We take it very seriously and not seriously at all. Chili cook-offs are part of many annual festivals in Texas, and there are major competitions, like the ones at Terlingua and San Marcos, where the cook-off is the festival. Humor and showmanship abound at the cook-offs, and their popularity has encouraged supporters of other traditional foods to organize cook-offs of their own—for *menudo* (tripe soup) and *frijoles* (pinto beans).

TAMALES

The tamale, unlike chili, is unquestionably Mexican and does not have a cow camp origin myth. (The singular is sometimes given as *tamal* in Spanish but usually *tamale* in Texan.) Like chili, this dish deserves special attention because the version eaten in Texas is uniquely Tex-Mex, yet its origins are ancient. An early version probably was made by the Aztecs, and the corn and corn shucks that are indispensable in making tamales are definitely New World contributions. However, the Tex-Mex version depends on a stuffing of pork or beef from the cattle and pigs that were introduced by the Spaniards. And unlike the tamales of Mexico, which are prepared with a variety of fillings including sweet ones, the tamale on the Tex-Mex menu is stuffed only with a spicy meat filling. The traditional stuffing of Christmas tamales, which are prepared as a sort of seasonal open-house treat, is ground pork from a boiled hog's head. Processed cornmeal called *masa harina* is used to make the *masa* (dough) for stuffing (the cornmeal may also be called simply masa). Spiced broth from the boiled meat, salt, and a little chili powder season the masa, which is cooked and then worked with lard. The masa is spread thinly on prepared corn shucks and spread with the ground meat mixture, then the shucks are rolled up and the tamales are steamed till done (a half hour or more). Making dozens of tamales is an assembly-line process and is best undertaken, like a quilting bee, as a social occasion.

The time and effort involved in making tamales, plus the fact that really good ones have long been available from vendors (and now from the local grocery store), is an aspect of the tamale's unique place on the Tex-Mex menu: tamales are eaten almost as commonly as chili, but most cooks who are not Mexican-Americans do not make their own at home. (Important exceptions to this rule, and a testament to the multicultural heritage of Texas, are the many African-American Texans who have been tamale chefs par excellence.) As the population becomes more mobile and fewer people live near their extended families, and as more women enter the work force, more Mexican-American cooks also prefer to buy rather than prepare tamales.

THE MEXICAN PLATE

Among the combination dinners on the Tex-Mex restaurant menu should be one called the Mexican Plate. It contains chili-covered enchiladas or tamales (or both), refried beans, and Spanish rice. A Tex-Mex enchilada consists of a chopped onion and grated cheese mixture rolled in a tortilla and covered with chili (sometimes topped with more cheese); this is heated in the oven till the cheese melts and is then served immediately. Lots of melted cheese is a primary characteristic of Tex-Mex cooking. Refried beans (*frijoles refritos*) are cooked pinto beans mashed, seasoned, and refried in lard. Spanish rice is seasoned with tomato paste, chili powder, and cumin.

Tostadas (fried corn tortillas) and salsa (or picante sauce) may be served before the main course begins. Heated corn tortillas have traditionally been served with Tex-Mex food, but flour tortillas are rapidly surpassing the original flat corn breads in popularity, even in such traditional places as the Presidio area. Tacos, chalupas, chile con queso, and guacamole are acceptable side dishes, and either a pecan praline or sherbet may be offered for dessert. These are the dishes that can be found in many "home cooking" cafes around the state, along with other standard fare such as chicken fried steak, fried chicken, fried catfish, and barbecue. These are also the foods most commonly prepared in non–Mexican-American homes.

The typical Tex-Mex menu, like many other regional aspects of American life, has been affected by the increased movement of the population and the communications explosion that has occurred since the 1940s. The development of national chain restaurants, especially fast-food chains, has, ironically, fostered both change and standardization. As more Americans eat Mexican food in a chain restaurant in New York or Chicago, the more they expect Mexican food in the Southwest to taste like what they are used to. And if a burrito is garnished with ripe olives in California, so should it be in Texas. Milder chili and chile sauces are even being served in many places in Texas because so many palates have been educated elsewhere.

Despite these pernicious influences, not all of the changes occurring in the Tex-Mex menu are the result of nontraditional intrusions. Some of the "new" dishes have long been cooked in Mexican-American homes but were not necessarily found in restaurants. Good examples of this phenomenon are burritos and fajitas, both now familiar items across the state. Burritos are simply soft tacos made with flour tortillas. Favorite fillings include a scrambled egg and chile mixture, egg and potato, refried beans, and carne guisada.

Fajitas, soft tacos filled with strips of marinated and grilled flank steak, are a reflection of the economic choice that has given rise to many excellent home-cooked meals around the world: choose a cheaper, and usually tougher, cut of meat and find a delicious way to cook it. Today, fajitas have become one of the most popular—and expensive—items on the Tex-Mex menu. They have become so popular that national food chains have even developed fajita off-shoots such as the chicken fajita (a contradiction in terms, since fajita refers to the flank steak) or the fajita pita which substitutes Middle Eastern pita bread for the tortilla.

Of course, there have long been restaurants in the larger Texas cities that serve a much broader selection of traditional dishes than the "Mexican Plate." Some common items on these extended menus are chile relleno, chicken con mole, and corn guisada. And, in Hispanic neighborhoods, there are the many restaurants that offer Hispanic "home cooking," where one finds dishes like menudo (a tripe soup made with either *pozole*-type corn or hominy) and even *cabrito* (young goat), baked in the oven (*al horno*, for the traditional outdoor oven) or cooked on a spit over coals (*al pastor*, or as the shepherds cooked it).

BREAD AND BREAKFAST

Wheat flour, one of the Old World foods imported to the New World, has been put to good use by Mexican-American cooks, not only in flour tortillas (now being made in a whole wheat version) and delicious crusty rolls called *bolillos*, but also in delicious sweet rolls. The term *pan dulce* (literally *sweet bread*) describes several sweet rolls that are great for breakfast with café con leche. Wherever you find a good Mexican bakery (*panadería*), you will find the pan dulces, *empanadas* (little fried pastries stuffed with fruit preserves or pumpkin), and several kinds of cookies. The favorites of children usually are the pig-shaped gingerbread cookies called *marranitos*. *Buñuelos* (fried, sweet flour tortillas, sprinkled with cinnamon and sugar) are related to *sopapillas*, which are now common in restaurants. Sopapilla pastry is fried so that it puffs up rapidly and steam forms a hollow shell in the center, ideal for holding the honey that is usually served as an accompaniment.

Those who like a heartier, less continental breakfast will find the Tex-Mex egg dishes more filling: *huevos rancheros* (eggs served with a tomato and pepper sauce, very hot), *migas* (eggs scrambled with corn tortillas, cheese, and onions), and *huevos con chorizo* (eggs scrambled with Mexican sausage). The Spanish omelet, however, should be viewed with suspicion by those in search of traditional dishes, since it is usually indistinguishable from a creole omelet or an American version sometimes called a Western omelet. Much more in keeping with the Tex-Mex tradition is the simple practice of pouring chili over scrambled eggs or simply covering fried eggs with picante sauce. Hearty Tex-Mex egg dishes are especially popular for weekend brunches, rather than as early morning breakfasts.

MEMORIES

Many people who have grown up in Texas share fond memories associated with their favorite Tex-Mex foods. A simple dish of tamales may serve as a reminder of almost forgotten neighbors and their offerings of friendship on Christmases past. Conjunto music on the radio may stir memories of Diez y Seis carnivals and *aguas frescas*—cool, fruit-flavored drinks served from large glass-jar dispensers. The mechanized tinkle of an ice-cream truck may recall to older Texans a time when *la raspa* (fruit-flavored, shaved ice, like a snow cone) could still be purchased from ancient horse-drawn ice-cream carts. Then there were little neighborhood grocery stores in almost every block, many of them just small shops in the fronts of peoples' homes, and they sold chorizo and bologna, penny candy and the red, green, and white striped coconut candy from Mexico. The spicy aroma of food booths at a fiesta may once again transport us back to those days of our childhood, recalling the vivid spring green of *nopalitos* and grass and the laughter of childhood friends. Or those memories may be sparked by the vivid blues and greens of a painting of nopalito harvesting by Carmen Lomas Garza, remembered from her South Texas childhood. The memories we share are part of the heritage we share.

Fire on the Furrow:
Salsa Wars and Other Battles on
the New Chile Frontier

Kent Ian Paterson

Held every February in an echoey ballroom in Albuquerque's Convention Center, the Fiery Foods extravaganza sets ablaze the drab interior of the downtown hall. On stage is a cast of salsa wizards, chile picklers, *mole* manufacturers, and anyone else inclined to tickle the taste buds of spice seekers. The show is *the* place to grab a look at—and a hot bite of—the latest trends in the industry.

Behind a booth, a large man puts bottles of Louisiana hot sauce in paper bags for customers. "It is so wonderful, it is so good, that I have old-time Cajuns write me letters and say it's a lot easier to buy from you in the bottle than have my wife try to make it . . . *Playboy* picked that as the best picante in the world, they tested over 300," he bellows. Dick Chileen and sister-in-law Maria give samples of their chile beer. Residents of tiny Cave Creek, Arizona, they hatched the brew in 1991 at Ed and Maria Chileens's restaurant The Satisfied Frog. Asked about the name, Maria, cracking a smile, replies that there was already a restaurant down the road called the Horny Toad, and the Chileens decided they would rather be a "satisfied frog than a horny toad." The beer, which is topped with a serrano chile, was originally meant for the restaurant, but news spread, and by 1993 the Chileens were shipping 25,000 cases a month including 2,000 to Japan and England. They had orders waiting to be filled for the Caribbean and Europe. "It's going like gangbusters," remarks Ed.

In 1993, the biggest hit at the show was the habanero pepper, the world's hottest, or the "real McCoy" as one professor—turned Virgin Islands sauce seller—put it. That was good news to one man decked out in an old green army jacket and sweating profusely in the face. "I'm a habanero buff," he brags. "That's probably the hottest pepper there is and I'm addicted to these, so I keep coming back to the habanero tables time and time again."

Kent Ian Paterson, "Fire on the Furrow: Salsa Wars and Other Battles on the New Chile Frontier," from *The Hot Empire of Chile*. Arizona State University, Tempe, AZ: Bilingual Press/Editorial Bilinge, 2000. Used by permission.

To prove the versatility of chile and its use in many other products besides food, Robert Schneider of Southwest Ventures had a display featuring "Body Guard," a cayenne-based self-defense spray effective in warding off attackers, animal or human. On the display table were testimonials from SWAT team members, harried drivers, and pitbull-dogged joggers swearing to the utility of the spray. A Californian, Schneider himself keeps a canister on the right-turn signal of his truck. "With all the car-jackings going on, I try to keep it handy there." The "Body Guard" product is a good illustration of how the chile business touches many facets of life, as a food, a condiment, a food-coloring agent, a cosmetic ingredient, a medicine, and a weapon. Brave, new industrial uses await the chile producer.

Keeping a close tab on these trends was Dave DeWitt, the brains behind the Fiery Foods shindig and editor of a magazine dedicated to the capsicum appropriately titled *Chile Pepper*, the bible of the hard-core chilehead. Before it was sold off to a publishing group in Texas, the magazine kept watch on the ups and downs (mostly ups) of the industry from an Albuquerque office. Reaching a circulation of 70,000 within just a few years, the publication began by a fluke in 1987.

DeWitt, a New Mexico chile lore author, approached publisher Robert Siegel with the idea of putting out a one-time catalog of chile products. Buyers assumed the catalog was a magazine and sent blank checks to the publisher. "And it just sort of took off," recalled DeWitt. "It was just one of those weird things, without any organization, without a business plan, with a very small office, without any backers, without any operating stock, without a fleet of cars or anything, we started a magazine." Five years and dozens of issues later, *Chile Pepper* boasted fans worldwide and cosponsored California rock concerts headlined by luminaries such as Carlos Santana and Sammy Hagar, an achievement realized by the luck of the pepper. The most visible boom was in hot sauces, salsas, and picante sauces. By 1990, hot sauce sales in U.S. supermarkets nudged $60 million, not counting restaurants and processing uses in popular foods like the Buffalo Wing. The chile was mainly produced in New Mexico and Latin America, but was made into hot sauce in the old Louisiana market corner. Of course, McIlhenny Company was at the pinnacle of the hot sauce phenomenon.

In its early years, the Louisiana hot sauce business was highly competitive, hosting a lineup of companies such as B. F. Trappey's, which gave the Tabasco-mashing McIlhenny's a serious knockdown challenge for the championship. The McIlhenny Company jabbed back by embarking on a relentless campaign to claim the trademark for the Tabasco pepper and pursued decades of court battles that paid off in 1948 when a Louisiana court ruled that the family-run business had a proprietary right to the Tabasco name. The zealousness with which the hot sauce maker has guarded the label is well documented in Amal Naj's book *Peppers: A Story of Hot Pursuits*. After the court win, McIlhenny Company and chief rival Trappey's duked it out in the stores for years, only ending the slugfest when Trappey's called it quits and sold off its gloves to the opponent.

A family enterprise of about 60 shareholders, McIlhenny pours out its sauce in the idyllic surroundings of Avery Island, Louisiana, amid the flight of egrets, the grunt of alligators, and the stony silence of a Buddhist shrine once given to a Chinese emperor. Enjoying more than $50 million in annual sales of merchandise encompassing pepper-flavored jellies, jalapeños, and "Cajun Chic" novelties, McIlhenny Company is perpetually on the make for new markets and has penetrated former Eastern Bloc countries like the Baltic States. "Sales have grown compoundly," says Paul McIlhenny, the company's vice president, matter-of-factly.

In 1990 the contest was virtually over. McIlhenny had 33 percent of the hot sauce market, 11 points over its nearest competitor, Durkee French Foods; it sold its products in more than 100 countries; it was the semiofficial hot sauce of U.S. troops, and it won grander conquests as a condiment to astronauts' rations in outer space. These facts prompted one Cincinnati businessman to exclaim, "McIlhenny is laughing all the way to the bank."

The sales surge was even greater in the salsa and picante sauce business. Old El Paso, La Victoria, and Pace, the traditional royalty of the market, got some new competition from both expected and unexpected sources in the 1980s. Borden, Hormel, Frito-Lay, and Anheuser-Busch waded into the waters with their own sauces. Even the actor Paul Newman got into the act with his Newman's Own brand. Surely the only salsa company to donate all its profits to charities, Newman's Own touted its salsa in a poster showing the actor sitting in a jail cell in a scene harking back to *Butch Cassidy and the Sundance Kid*.

Salsa sales soared in the 1980s and 1990s, jumping from about $245 million in 1984 to about $700 million in 1993; by 1999 sales had reached $1.4 billion. Displays in supermarket aisles were often combined with tortilla chips, a marketing device that proved beneficial to both salsa and chips. More than 300 salsa and picante sauce brands were available in the U.S. market, running the gamut from handmade recipes to mass-produced household names.

Symbolizing the change in Americans' dietary preferences, salsa surpassed ketchup in sales in 1991. Recognizing the historic milestone, Heinz Company entered the salsa business in 1993, with a cross between salsa and ketchup. Michael Zakany of Zanesville, Ohio, was an example of the new small salsa entrepreneur. He ran José Madrid Products, named after his grandfather from Lincoln County, New Mexico. His original creations like Clovis Red sold in gourmet shops in the Midwest and other regions. "In a lot of areas, the grocery stores will only carry the national brands and the salsa consumer out there just wants something different, and therefore they will go to specialty stores and find my product," he explained. Nevertheless, the die was cast early on in the salsa world. "When this market matures, there will be no room for mediocre sauce makers or companies with small budgets," predicted Frank Smith of the Sami market research firm.

In 1989 several companies already had the bulk of the business. Vying for the championship were Old El Paso and Pace, both Texas-located companies using New Mexico chile and doling out a huge amount of picante sauce. Pace, the San Antonio giant, had a modest beginning in the 1940s in the rear of David Pace's liquor store, where the upstart chile blender bottled syrups, jellies, peppers, and pickles with the aid of his wife and a pair of employees.

In the days after sugar-starved World War II, Pace decided that the true future lay with his onion-tomato-jalapeño picante sauce, hardly a new creation but novel enough for the gringo taste to launch him onto the road to success. According to spokesman Matt Mohr, one early company oversight was the failure to trademark the word "picante sauce," a legality that could have done for Pace what the word "Tabasco" did for McIlhenny. No matter. Pace became a common shelf item in the 50 states, Canada, and Mexico, utilizing chile purchased on a "trail" that extended from New Mexico to the Yucatan Peninsula and from Florida to California. In 1989, Pace was the spicy condiment of choice at President Bush's inauguration. Pace workers were referred to as "associates," a term flowing from the company's philosophy of worker-management cooperation. Guiding the team were a powerhouse of food industry veterans, drawn from the likes of Uncle Ben's Rice, Anderson-Clayton, Kraft Foods, General Mills, and Church's Fried Chicken. Pace and chief rival Old El Paso succeeded in controlling about 50 percent of the salsa-picante market in 1991. Three years later Pace surpassed Old El Paso, gobbling up 26 percent of salsa sales versus 21 percent for the Mexican foods kingpin. Competitors such as Pepsico's Frito-Lay, La Victoria, RJR-Nabisco's Ortega, and Hormel's Chi Chi's lagged behind but were making strenuous efforts to catch up or at least make a respectable showing at the finish line. The corporations spent generous sums on advertising, reaching more than $20 million in 1986, with three of the contenders for the salsa crown, Pace, Old El Paso, and Ortega, equaling that amount in 1991. Pace engaged La Victoria in an advertising war on La Victoria's home turf in California, which was conducted in an almost gentlemanly way compared with the truly nasty rivalry that broke out between Pace and Old El Paso. Like two crusty old gunslingers facing off at high noon for the fifteenth time, the companies waged a no-holds-barred shootout as they fired away at each other with an arsenal of insulting television ads and lawsuits.

Mythical western imagery was included in the firms' ads, associating salsa with the old Wild West. Oddly, a Pace product, Territorial House Salsa, had a history that was really related to the new violent West. A New Mexico favorite, Territorial House was first made by a family that ran the old Territorial House restaurant in Corrales, New Mexico, situated in a building where hangings were reputed to have occurred in the last century. The "T-House's" owner, a former New Mexico state policeman, went down in a blaze of gunfire in the mid-1970s. In a still mysterious shooting incident, the ex-cop confronted two men in the bar's parking lot and let loose a staccato of rifle fire at them, killing the two and then breaking the butt of his rifle on their bodies. The man walked back into the bar-restaurant and collapsed 45 minutes later. He was dead of a heart attack.

In 1986, Pace, upset at an Old El Paso ad resembling a Pace jingle and infuriated at an Old El Paso salsa jar seemingly copied from Pace's, filed against the St. Louis–based company in San Antonio's U.S. District Court, requesting that Old El Paso cease using the bottle. Pace president Kit Goldsbury charged that his longstanding rival had implemented a secret plan called "Project Pace-Like," a clandestine operation allegedly involving attempts to pry information from Pace employees and from the San Antonio company's garbage. The two salsa makers settled out of court in 1987, Old El Paso scuttled the bottle, and the contenders returned to their television jousts. One Old El Paso ad, for instance, implied that Pace's sauce was akin to a watery soup and upheld Old El Paso as the "taste that runs wild," while Pace simply "just runs."

Eventually, the stakes were raised to a possibly deciding hand in the Pace/Old El Paso rivalry. Late in 1994, Campbell's Soups, a company with a sales base about six times that of Pet's, trumpeted the deal of the century in the salsa-chile business. After three years of secret negotiations, Campbell's announced it was purchasing Pace for a whopping $1.1 billion. For Pace, the sale closed the book on what was once a penny-ante, back-room kitchen concoction whipped into a billion-dollar bonanza. Pace head Kit Goldsbury, who had risen to the top through marriage to David Pace's daughter and the earlier buyout of both his former father-in-law and spouse, was vaulted into the Fortune 500 list. In the wake of the Pace sell-off, the business magazine estimated Goldsbury's personal fortune at around $900 million.

The buyout added Pace products to Campbell's growing line of chile-related foods: Vlasic peppers, chile poblano soup, and Fiesta tomato soup. While the Pace buyout was admittedly an expensive splurge on the part of a company with a relatively conservative record of business practices, it forced the main players in the salsa race, especially Old El Paso, into a do-or-die position considering Campbell's name recognition in supermarkets and the firm's access to the global consumer.

The Pace-Campbell's deal foretold a redoubled scramble for markets, leaner production methods, and cheaper-source chile. By entering a business in the throes of a contest for monopoly champion, and by doing it with a sweepstakes ticket bought at scalper's rates, Campbell's was certainly engaging in a daring risk. But by using an arguably strange accounting loophole that granted tax breaks for acquisitions on the basis of a name's "value," which in this case corresponded to Pace's reputation in the dip 'n' chip realm, Campbell's stood to gain a $200 million tax deduction for the deal. Certainly the soup and salsa chefs were putting their bets on Pace's familiarity and favorable consumer trends. As the company's own ad boasted, "Never underestimate the power of Campbell's."

Apparently, Pet was not minimizing Campbell's. Under the new economic circumstances, it was inevitable that the St. Louis–based food company would once again fall to the global tidal wave of corporate buyouts. After a winter of courting from the likes of England's Grand Metropolitan, ConAgra, and H. J. Heinz, Pet and its Old El Paso Foods division were sold to the British company in early 1995 for the staggering sum of $2.65 billion. The sale represented the fourth instance since the 1960s that the onetime El Paso–owned company was put on the auction block. Old El Paso was next put under the management of Grand Metropolitan's Pillsbury foods, which itself had been acquired by the conglomerate in 1988 in a deal that landed one Minnesota lawyer in court for earning a $4 million profit from insider trading. Grand Metropolitan, which later signed a $15.8 billion merger with the brewing company Guinness to form the seventh largest food and beverage company in the world (Diageo, Inc.), now counted Burger King, Häagen-Dazs, Green Giant, and Pillsbury among its holdings. The conglomerate was boycotted by labor unions and sympathizers in the early 1990s when its Green Giant division shut down a Watsonville, California, broccoli-processing plant and moved it to the cheaper labor quarters of Irapuato, Mexico. Unconcerned, Grand Metropolitan ran a food empire based on the trendiest delectables of the times: fast, frozen, sweet, and spicy. Henceforth, the Pace–Old El Paso salsa wars would strictly be the business of global titans.

True to form, Old El Paso performed for Pillsbury much as it had for Pet. One year after the acquisition, Old El Paso was contributing nicely to Pillsbury's profits, taking in $353 million from salsa sales in 1996 alone. In other categories, Old El Paso could boast at being *Número Uno* in the nation's rising Mexican foods business. The firm held the lead in seasoning mix and dinner kit sales, inventing the one-skillet Mexican dinner that delivered a meal to hungry customers in a quick 20 minutes. Old El Paso's flag touched the shores of Europe, Australia, Canada, South America, and Asia. A chara-cter, "Nacho Man," was created to ensure consumer identification with both a popular product and an individual company.

But Old El Paso's future was being shaped far from its original home on the Rio Grande. From the Twin Cities, a 20-person Pillsbury team coordinated company strategies. None of the team members was Mexican or Latino. One culinary observer noted an iconization in progress. "The food that is being manufactured by Pillsbury and Hormel is not really Mexican food," said Food Processing magazine editor Bob Messenger. "We basically shook the culture out of pasta. We're doing the same to Mexican food."

Grand Metropolitan's Pillsbury, reflecting the lean and mean ethos of the times, then devised a clever way to squeeze even greater profit out of Old El Paso Foods. In June 1997, the company announced the sale of its Anthony fac-tory for an undisclosed price to a group of Denver-based investors including businessman Jim Lewis. Despite the sale, Grand Met/Pillsbury wasn't willing to part completely with a bulging cash cow. As part of the agreement, Pills-bury retained the trademark rights to Old El Paso for seven years. The name was so valuable that Pillsbury could contract out production while reap-ing dividends from the actual store sales. In explaining the deal, Pillsbury officials described the sale as "consistent with an ongoing strategy to reduce fixed assets and to lower costs." Ultimately, the innovation added another link in the payoff chain from producer to distributor. The new plant owner named itself Anthony Foods, a division of Santa Fe Ingredients, which itself was under the JELTEX umbrella formed to leverage agribusiness companies. While producing for Pillsbury, Anthony Foods also custom packed for labels such as Clover Club and Dillon Foods. In serving its clients, Anthony Foods was able to make far more product with far fewer people. From a figure of 800 full-time and 1,200 to 1,300 seasonal (chile pack) employees in about 1977, the number of workers dipped to 250 full-time and 400 to 600 seasonal employees twenty years later. Although ownership changed numerous times and auto-mation slashed the workforce, the historic Mountain Pass cannery continued shipping massive amounts of chile-based Mexican foods the world over.

Whether as a condiment or as cayenne spray, chile was a much coveted commodity. Per capita use of chile peppers in the United States nearly doubled from 3.5 pounds per person a year in 1980 to 6.5 pounds per person by the early 1990s. An herb industry trade publication pointed to the shifting preference for ethnic foods such as Mexican as being responsible for the surge. In a milestone of sorts, retail sales of Mexican foods almost hit the $3 billion mark in 1999, portending a brisk business in the coming century.

As sales skyrocketed, technological innovations were introduced, always with the same goal of eliminating extra labor and increasing profits. Companies thought of using electrical energy to peel chile more efficiently and reduce the amount of lost, exploded pods wasted in the steam-roasting method, and processes were developed to rapidly remove red chile stems. Rudderless after the Cold War, even New Mexico's Los Alamos National Laboratories (LANL) got involved. The mission: to automate the troublesome business of picking out the teeny-weeny pieces of chile skin stuck to peeled, roasted pods. LANL scientists investigated ways of using laser scanners to identify the remaining bits of peel on chiles rolling down the canning line. A successful device would rid a cannery's owners of the need to employ 40 people to inspect each pod by hand. Of course, not every breakthrough needed to be as high tech, and NMSU researchers tried finding ways of packaging fresh New Mexican green chiles for a longer shelf life and export to new markets. New Mexican chile, indeed, was almost everywhere in the heyday of the chile bonanza. What was troubling to some New Mexicans was that the state was not reaping the full benefits. The main processors—Pet's Old El Paso, Beatrice's Cal-Compack, Basic American Foods' Joy Canning, and others—were all owned by out-of-staters. Profits flowed to St. Louis, San Francisco, Chicago, and Baltimore. NMSU economist Robert Coppedge compared New Mexico's chile economy to a colonial one in which a raw product is extracted, processed elsewhere, and even sold back to the source country in a finished form—of course at a very high price. Furthermore, it was difficult for small New Mexican processors to get onto the grocery shelves of stores in their own state. Up-front payments were sometimes required. Several out-of-state chains—Albertson's, Smith's, Furr's, and others—crowded the landscape. They serviced large numbers of customers, were supplied by big distributors, and dealt in nationally recognized products. On occasion, outright conflict broke out between local and national processors. When McCormick's Mojave Foods bid for exclusive space in Furr's Supermarkets in 1993, Bueno Food's Jackie Baca went to war to keep her company's chile on sale at the chain.

Consequently, one NMSU study claimed the absurd statistic that 95 percent of the processed Mexican food purchased in New Mexico, the country's largest chile producer and per capita consumer, was imported from out of state. A diner could stumble into a Las Cruces barbecue joint and find a bottle of Louisiana-bottled hot sauce that was most likely heated with Mesilla Valley chiles. It was in the "value-added" segment of the chile industry that the most money was earned. For example, the farm-gate value of New Mexico chile (the amount sold by the farmers) was about $88 million in 1991 compared to the value-added amount of between $230 and $300 million that same year.

New Mexico's neighbor to the east and the south, Texas, noticed the vibrant chile industry up the Rio Grande and decided to give the Land of Enchantment a run for its chile, setting off the "Texas–New Mexico Chile War," surely one of the most ingenious marketing schemes of the modern U.S. food industry. In 1992 Texas's 5,000 acres of hot peppers put the Lone Star State far behind New Mexico, but Texas had lots of potential. For one thing, the Texas Department of Agriculture aggressively promoted its producers and processors in a "Taste of Texas" campaign that matched interested buyers with a computer data-base of sellers. Two growing seasons, in contrast to New Mexico's one, blessed the Rio Grande Valley of south Texas, where a jalapeño industry took shape. Other production areas included the Texas Panhandle, the "Hill Country" between San Antonio and Austin, and, of course, El Paso County just south of the New Mexico chile belt. Texas also had a chile-breeding research program second only to New Mexico's at the Texas A&M agricultural experiment station in Weslaco—the laboratory of Dr. Ben Villalón. Favored with fertile soils, varying climates, and, in some areas, virgin lands unspoiled by the chile wilt disease, Texas farmers planted more than 100 varieties, ranging from hot Thai to jalapeño varieties.

Jeff Campbell, a Hill Country farmer and the owner of the Stonewall Chili Pepper Company, grew 40 acres of many different peppers. His most popular was the habanero, the world's hottest, and he doubled his plantings between 1992 and 1993. "Everybody's habanero crazy," he asserted. "Certain chiles, like the habanero . . . like a higher humidity; it's a very tropical chile, that's why I think it grows well here."

The opening shot of the "Texas–New Mexico Chile War" was fired in August 1992 by Hill Rylander, the proprietor of the Austin Farmer's Market. In a brazen challenge, Rylander told the press he was "tired" of New Mexico's claim to be the chile leader, and he proceeded to sponsor the first annual Texas Chile Festival in Austin on the same weekend as the Hatch Chile Festival. The Texas event drew thousands and featured the christening of a Texas chile capital statue. Rylander's bold challenge aroused old New Mexican fears of Texan colonization, which dated back to the 1800s. Then a would-be Texan conquering force got lost in the desert and was rounded up by Mexican soldiers. The fears survived into the present century and are exemplified by a Santa Fe County bumper sticker that reads "Welcome to Aztlán: Now Go Home." New Mexican reactions to the Texas festival were amusing. "Texans are the world's greatest bullhorns, they claim they can grow crawdads better than the Louisianans, chile better than the New Mexicans," chortled Gordon Brown, the co-owner of Bruce Foods. "Texas is my neighbor," said farmer Robert Cosimati. "They grow everything big in Texas, including their mouths."

In response, the City Council of El Paso declared the first chile war cook-off for El Paso in 1993 and promised to storm Santa Fe if New Mexico did not cease its rhetoric about being the world's chile capital. In turn, New Mexico set its own chile war cook-off for Las Cruces, inviting the Texans in for a match on the New Mexican turf, and when New Mexico Speaker of the House Raymond Sánchez appeared before legislators in Santa Fe at the 1993 session,

he crowned a pepper and proclaimed the Land of Enchantment's chile
supremacy. It was all in jest, of course—at least most of it.

On a truly competitive note, Texas, New Mexico, and other states vied with
each other for new processing facilities, offering tax breaks and other incen-
tives for plants to relocate. Wes Grable, owner of the popular Southwestern
Piada brand of picante sauce, got calls from the New Mexico Department of
Economic Development, which tried to lure him away from his home base
in rural Texas. Over in Deming, Arnold Orquiz, the proprietor of Amigo's
Foods, received similar queries from at least eight states but decided to stay
in New Mexico after the state government stepped in to rescue his business.
Apparently, Orquiz's arguments about saving jobs for the Deming community and the future potential of his growing business with Mexico convinced
the state to make a direct investment in his food-processing firm. "There's
a giant on the other side of the border and you guys are sleeping," Orquiz
told officials including Governor King. Competition in the chile business
from other states and countries prodded New Mexico officials to take a long,
strategic look at not only preserving the industry, but making sure it stayed
number one as well. The involvement of NMSU was critical to achieving
this goal, and the school made plans to assume an even bigger role in chile.
Dr. Bosland teamed up with Dave DeWitt of *Chile Pepper* magazine to
launch the Chile Institute, headquartered at NMSU. The Institute declared
ambitious goals: its intent was to keep New Mexico the *chile grande* through
enhanced pepper breeding, education, and even the opening of a museum
dedicated to chile peppers.

Bosland also conceived of the Institute as the main international deposi-
tory of chile germplasm, a responsibility he regarded as vital in light of the
disappearance of chile species caused by the destruction of the tropical rain-
forests. One of those species, he pointed out, might have been the successful
cross-breed of a wilt-resistant variety, or even an invaluable aid in fighting
cancer and other diseases.

The NMSU-based Chile Institute drew financial support from both the
State of New Mexico and private food-processing corporations. Five of those
companies—Bueno, Border Foods, Biad, Cervantes Enterprises, and Pet/
Old El Paso—were represented on the Institute's Board of Directors. The
Chile Institute was officially announced at the NMSU-sponsored 1992 Chile
Conference at Las Cruces Hilton Hotel, where hundreds of growers and processors from as far away as Wisconsin hobnobbed in the hallways and lobby
and heard presentations about free trade, fungus control, and opportunities
in paprika.

Inside the hotel, attendees lunched with staff members from Senator
Domenici and Senator Binghaman's offices, who were present to show their
bosses' unyielding support for the New Mexico chile industry. Outside, it
was an entirely different scene altogether. About 50 pickets from the Border
Agricultural Workers Union stood on a sidewalk in front of the Hilton and
conducted a loud, vocal demonstration for higher wages and improved working conditions. "We want them to pay us more, to pay us better," commented
one picket, who described his picking job as *agachado*, or bent over, all day

long. "If you work seven to eight hours they'll [labor contractors] put down three to four hours. They pay you for four hours," he charged.

After chanting slogans for a good spell, the workers huddled together to wait for union director Carlos Marentes to return from the hotel. Marentes entered the conference in an attempt to address the farmers who employed the labor contractors. He was out of luck: the agenda already had been set, he was told. Marentes walked back to the picket line and told the workers he would not be speaking to the growers. But he was not surprised at the rebuff. "The role of the university here in Las Cruces is to support the production, to help them find ways to make the chile farm productive every time. But see, the only way they can make more profits from chile is to pay less to the workers and [by] avoiding benefits other workers enjoy. Now we hear about all this money from the federal government and the State of New Mexico going into the pockets of farmers, and basically the chile industry, and not a single penny for the benefit of the farmworkers, or not a single penny to alleviate the situation [farmworkers] are facing."

In front of the Hilton, with the volcano-coned Picacho Peak lording over the morning haze of the Valley, stood Gloria Escovedo. She was hurting, but she felt compelled to be on the picket line that day. "I'm a farmworker, I was a farmworker, and I support the union for better wages, so that there will be justice," said Escovedo. "It's an injustice that [farmworkers] don't get paid what they should earn. They should put bathrooms [in the fields], have better salaries, and be fair to us farmworkers that make the least."

Undeterred, the protesting chile pickers wrapped up their red union flags and boarded their bus for El Paso. The 1992 harvest season had not yet started, and many workers faced several more months of unemployment or underemployment before the pickings would be good. The union temporarily settled back into its routine work, priming itself for the fall harvest when its demands would resurface. Once again, conflict was brewing in chile country.

NOTES

There are no corresponding note numbers in the text as this is how it appeared in the original.

1. Dick Chileen and Maria Chileen, interviews by author, Albuquerque, NM, February 1993.

2. Robert Schneider, interview by author, Albuquerque, NM, February 1993.

3. Dave DeWitt, telephone conversation with author, August 1991.

4. "Hot, hot, hot," *The Times-Picayune* (New Orleans), 24 June 1990.

5. Dana Wechsler Linden, "Hot Stuff," *Forbes*, 26 November 1990, 164–66.

6. Amal Naj, *Peppers: A Story of Hot Pursuits* (New York: Alfred A. Knopf, 1992).

7. For an overview of the McIlhenny Co., see Diane M. Moore, *The Treasures of Avery Island* (Lafayette, LA: Acadian House Publishing, 1990); "Tabasco-Sauce Maker Remains Hot after 125 Years," *The Wall Street Journal*, 11 May 1990; Patricia Mandell, "Louisiana Hot," *Americana*, February 1991, 26-31.

8. Paul McIlhenny, telephone conversation with author, August 1992.

9. William Updike, Eagle Salsa/Anheuser Busch, telephone conversation with author, June 1992.

10. Todd McKenzie, Frito Lay, telephone conversation with author, June 1992.

11. Mary Barinka and Richard Crane, Hormel, telephone conversations with author, July 1992.

12. Linda Rohr, Newman's Own, telephone conversations with author, June 1992.

13. "Food Industry's War of the Salsas Is Getting Fierce," *Wall Street Journal*, 11 April 1989.

14. David Weiss, Packaged Facts, telephone conversation with author, July 1992.

15. *Fiery Foods and Barbeque Business Magazine*, July/August 1999.

16. Michael Zakany, interview by author, Albuquerque, NM, February 1993.

17. *Advertising Age*, 19 July 1993, 8.

18. "Pet Peeves Pace with Parallel Picante Packaging," *Albuquerque Journal*, 17 May 1987.

19. *Albuquerque Journal*, 29 December 1991.

20. "Campbell picks up Pace in hot market," *USA Today*, 29 November 1994; *Fiery Foods!*, March 1995, 5.

21. *Fortune* Web site.

22. *Minneapolis Star Tribune*, 21 February 1995; *Twin Cities Business Monthly*, July 1995; *St. Paul Pioneer Press*, 17 May 1996; *Minneapolis–St. Paul City Business Journal*, 3 February 1997, 19 May 1997, 30 June 1997, 29 December 1997; Pillsbury/Old El Paso Web site, Pillsbury press release, 25 June 1997; telephone conversations with Tom La Hut, Anthony Foods, 8 June 1998, and Ramón Coral, United Food and Commercial Workers Union, El Paso, TX, 1 June 1998.

23. *Fiery Foods and Barbeque Business Magazine* Web site.

24. Arlene Cinelli Odenwald, "Rural Economic Development: The Issues," *New Mexico Business Journal*, August 1992, 24.

25. *New Mexico Technology Enterprise Forum*, January-February 1994, 3.

26. Kip Smith, interview by author, Hatch, NM, September 1992.

27. *New Mexico Resources*, spring 1992; *Albuquerque Journal*, Business Outlook, 4 May 1992.

28. Valerie J. Gerard, "Technology Enterprise Division Helps Las Cruces Pasta Business," *New Mexico Technology Enterprise Forum*, September-October 1992, 2.

29. *New Mexico Business Journal*, October 1991.

30. "Taste of Texas Companies," Texas Department of Agriculture, 1992; Mark Ellison, TDA, telephone conversation with author, August 1992.

31. Jeff Campbell, interview by author, Albuquerque, NM, February 1993.

32. "Texas Growers Pepper N.M. with Insults," *Albuquerque Journal*, 21 July 1992.

33. Hill Rylander, telephone conversation with author, September 1992.

34. Gordon Brown, Bruce Foods, telephone conversation with author, August 1992.

35. Robert Cosimati, interview by author, Las Cruces, NM, July 1992.

36. "Texas Fires First Festive Salvo in Chile War with New Mexico," Associated Press wire story, 17 December 1992.

37. "State Accepts Chile Challenge," Associated Press wire story, n.d.

38. *Las Cruces Sun-News*, 16 March 1993.

39. Wes Grable, telephone conversation with author, June 1992.

40. Arnold Orquiz, interview by author, Deming, NM, July 1992.

41. Paul Bosland, interview by author, Hatch, NM, August 1991.

42. Chile Institute informational brochure, NMSU, 1993.

43. Unnamed chile picker, interview by author, Las Cruces, NM, February 1992.

44. Carlos Marentes, interview by author, Las Cruces, NM, February 1992.

45. Gloria Escovedo, interview by author, Las Cruces, NM, February 1992.

Cooking with Chiles

Laura Esquivel

What Mexican hasn't eaten *chile*? Who hasn't gotten his fingers covered in *chile* juice? Who hasn't run the risk of smuggling a jar of *mole* or pickled *chiles* in his suitcase in hopes of continuing to enjoy the pleasure that *chile* gives its addicts? Who can remember the first time he felt his tongue burn, his forehead began to sweat, tears formed in his eyes, and his nose ran from eating *chiles*? No doubt it is very difficult to remember precisely because the *chile* is part of the ancestral memory of Mexicans and has been with us from time immemorial.

We know from the testimony of journalists that our indigenous forefathers ate *tortillas* and *tamales*, chickens and quails roasted with tomato, ground pumpkin seeds, and *chile*, and that they also ate a lot of dishes made from *chile*: a form of *chilmolli*, prepared with *chiltecpitl* and tomatoes, or with yellow *chile* and tomatoes, according to the words of Fray Bernadino de Sahagun in his *Historia General*. Nevertheless, even though they ate white or colored fishes, small or large birds, frogs or tadpoles, ants, tomatoes, corn in different forms, or pumpkin seeds, the preparation of the dishes was always accompanied by the flavor of *chile*. Be it red, yellow, green, in a round or elongated shape, or combined with *tortillas* and beans, the *chile* formed a fundamental part of the language, the flavor and the food of the old Mexicans. Independently of rank and social class, vegetables, fishes, meats, shrimp and insects needed to taste well seasoned and spicy. In fact, it is said that even at the tables of the poorest families there were various types of herbs, *nopal* cactus, beans, tomatoes, and inevitably a portion of *chile*.

The act of eating transcended the limits of the home and overflowed into the streets and markets. We know that in the *plazas*, for example, *tortillas*, *tamales*, *atole*, dishes of meat with *chile* and tomato, *mole*, *chilaquiles*, *chilmoles*, *pozole*, and stews of *nenepile* or *mesclapiques* were sold. It wasn't strange for travelers to carry pine nuts or sweet potato candies, roasted ears of corn, *jicama*, or some other fruit of the season generously covered with *chile*. At the same time, since those times, rural people have maintained in their diet foods for their arduous labors beneath the sun, and among these the *chile* was never absent.

The *chile* was also used in the practicing of magic and spell casting. The varieties with elongated shapes were associated with the masculine figure and the wider, rounder ones with the feminine. They were used to cleanse or as offerings so the good spirits could enjoy their benefits. They were burned to ward off evil spirits. They were used in rituals of thanksgiving, in ceremonies to deities of different orders and as medicinal plants. Because of their purging, disinfecting, and purifying properties they were used as poultices to alleviate swelling, or to cauterize, or as a pomade to cure stains on the skin, or even to facilitate the difficulties of birth and nursing.

Since remotest times there has not been an activity, public or private, profane or sacred, in Mexico where the presence of the *chile* has not been evident. Like a good guardian angel, it accompanies us always and does not forsake us night or day, in sickness or in health, in wealth or in poverty. Its influence in every area of our daily life is so powerful that it has survived the passage of time and all kinds of culinary influence. And so we modern Mexicans find ourselves continuing to eat exactly as our ancestors did, and each new food that has been included in our diet, we have made our own through the *chile*. From *bacalao* to hot dogs and hamburgers. Not only that, but we have also exported the *chile* to other cultures, and now there is talk of including the *chile* in the astronauts' diet.

A food staple, the *chile* has also invaded other orbits of our experience. It has become part of colloquial speech and has given a unique color to the expression of Spanish that is spoken in Mexico. Its use in speech is as diverse as its varieties and colors. It has meanings that range from clear and precise to vaguely implied and picaresque: *estar enchilado* (to be furious—a male); *estar enchilada* (to be furious—a female); *enchilarse* (to cover oneself—that is, one's fingers—with *chile*); *ser cuenta chiles* (to be a bean counter); *hablar al chile* (to talk meaninglessly).

The *chile*, then, forms a vital part of our daily alimentation, and there is no table on which it doesn't play a primary importance because its flavor is carried in our memory and in our blood, and its spiciness flows in our veins.

If one is what he eats, with whom he eats it, and how he eats it, then we can conclude that we Mexicans are children of corn, but we were formed of *chile*. I wonder whether the gods created us together or separately, and if the latter, which came first, man or the *chile*.

SAZÓN:

THE FLAVORS OF CULINARY EPISTEMOLOGY

Meredith E. Abarca

Irma: The rice needs to be fried, but only until it is light brown. Then, once the rice has reached its exact degree of frying, you just add the tomato sauce and water. Well, you have to know how much water to add, because if you add too much water the rice will have a watery texture. And if you do not add enough water, then the rice will not cook.

Maria Luisa: How do you know the amount of water?

Irma: Well, I think that is something you learn because I never measure anything. I just add water, and the rice comes out perfect. I guess I learned well. I feel it. I stir the water in the frying pan, and I know.

Meredith: You can calculate just by seeing the water, right?

Irma: No, I think it is in my hand because I just mix the rice [with a spoon] and I know when it needs more water or when it has enough. When I add the water, I stir it. I know. I don't know how I know. That, I could not explain to you.[1]

By using her hand as the measuring utensil, Irma Vásquez knows how much water she needs so her rice cooks to perfection. While confident in the efficiency of her *sazón*, a sensory way of knowing, Vásquez cannot explain the intrinsic logic of her touch. She only knows it works. Vásquez's sensory utensil, in this case her hand, reflects an epistemology based on the faculty of all of the senses: the *sazón*, the language spoken in the kitchen. Once practiced by individuals, the *sazón* becomes their culinary discourse to conceptualize and articulate aspects of their personal and social cultural environment. The kitchen and the *sazón* represent a form of a "sitio y lengua," to quote Emma Pérez, that offers a site of power (the kitchen) and

Meredith E. Abarca, *"Sazón*: The Flavors of Culinary Epistemology," from *Voices in the Kitchen: Views of Food and the World from Working-Class Mexican and Mexican American Women*. College Station: Texas A&M University Press, 2006. Used by permission of the Texas A&M University Press.

a discourse of empowerment (the *sazón*) to those historically silenced by colonialist, imperialist, and patriarchal social mechanisms.

Yet, finding ways to theorize the *sazón*'s conceptual process, a nonverbal cognitive logic, creates something of a challenge. Speaking metaphorically, a cook's *sazón* is like a gardener's green thumb. With this metaphor, we can understand that the *sazón* refers to the ability someone has to create a rather savory meal out of the simplest ingredients, just as a person with a green thumb can make anything grow. This metaphor, however, does not explain the ability a cook has to know *how* to create a meal out of the simplest ingredients. I am not referring here to the creative/artistic process of cooking. The question at hand is twofold: how do women guided by their senses, as Irma Vásquez says, know if a meal is cooking at the right temperature, if it has enough water, if it has enough salt; and how do their culinary epistemologies reveal personal aspects of their life stories?

What exactly is the *sazón*? Liduvina Vélez in a number of our *charlas* defines other people's *sazón* as "un don" (a gift some people are born with). For Imelda Silva, what contributes to other people's *buen sazón* is their ability to cook non-traditional working class Mexican meals. Talking about her cousin Alicia, Silva says, "My cousin taught me to make ham with pineapple. Macaroni salad. Ribs in barbecue sauce. These are things that I would have not learned because we don't eat them from where I come from. For me, my cousin was a very good cook. I considered her as a very good cook."[2] For Raquel Merlo, it is "la mano de la experiencia" (the hand of experience), and Erica Morales defines it as "el sazón de la mano" (a hand's knowledge).

If having a *sazón* is a gift, perhaps Liduvina Vélez's inclination to humility prevents her from seeing her own *buen sazón* as such. At the age of twenty-three when she sold food out of economic necessity, she says, "Sí tenía clientela. Nó sé, que les gustaba mi sazón. Malaya pare el sazón que haya tenido yo, pero sí les gustaba" (Yes, I had customers. I don't know, they liked my *sazón*. I don't think I had a good *sazón*, but they liked what I cooked). Modesty does not keep Vélez from seizing moments of agency by embracing her *buen sazón*. One of the few occasions in which she admits to having a good *sazón* is in the process of making masa for tortillas. When she speaks of making good tortillas, she expresses pride in her expertise. She shares this pride as she tells me how when she was first married, her sisters-in-law were rather surprised that she knew how to make tortillas by hand, from preparing the masa to serving warm tortillas in a basket: "Well, *mi'ja*, it has to do with knowing how to do something well. Even though I was not from the town, even though I came from where tortillas were not made at home, where you go and buy them, right, well [your father's sisters] were very surprised because they didn't believe that I would know how to make tortillas."[3] Throughout the *charlas*, this is one of the few times that Vélez openly admits to actually having *buen sazón*. The implication of the *sazón* as a *don* (gift) differs not only from one person to another, but at different periods of an individual's life, as is the case with Vélez.

Esperanza Vélez attributes her own "forma del buen sazón" (good ability to cook) to an external religious intervention. Whenever she adds salt to her meals, she says:

> When I add salt I take it with my fingers, [and] I say in the name of God, and add it to the food in the form of a cross. With my fingers, I can calculate perfectly. I always say, "in the name of God." I do it unconsciously. It's just a habit of mine. I always invoke God. He is either bless-ing my meals or my ability to calculate. I am so stupid [to cook well on my own] that I need to say, "in the name of God." It is something I do; no one taught me to do so. Maybe because I was so young when I started cooking in my aunt's house, I was about seven when my mother left me there. I had to use a stool, a little wooden chair to reach the stove and the pan. In the metate, I would grind tomatoes, or whatever was needed for the soup or other meals of the day. I think that this experience with my aunt is where the gesture of making the cross comes from. Maybe my fear of not doing things well was so strong because if I did things wrong my aunt would hit me. Therefore, unconsciously, I would say, "Oh, dear God, let this come out right." I used to have such fear! Only God could help me so that I would not fail in doing the recipe as my aunt had told me.[4]

In Esperanza Vélez's explanation of adding salt to food in the form of a cross, she conceptualizes and shares a personal aspect of childhood. The *sazón* in these particular moments of the *charlas* with Esperanza Vélez seems grounded in some source of divine intervention. Since *Voices* speaks about the knowledge these women reveal through our *charlas*, I believe it important to indicate that Esperanza Vélez introduces her "stupid" self-reference with laughter that she knows dismisses the potential claim that she lacks in her cooking abilities.

Her family and friends know Esperanza Vélez for her *forma de buen sazón*. For instance, she says, that while cooking frijoles is one of the simplest things to make, "todo el mundo dice que pa' frijoles los míos, nó" (everyone says that to eat good beans you must have mine, yes). Esperanza Vélez's self-assertiveness reflects her own belief in the abil-ity of her *sazón*. The culinary authority she derives from her *sazón* comes from years of recognition of her gastronomical talent, a recognition she receives from family and friends. Due to Esperanza Vélez's *sazón*, many people ask her to open a restaurant. "People have told me, 'you have a good *sazón*; why don't you open a food business?' No, I don't like that. For me, cooking for a restaurant, for people I don't know, is something I am not interested in doing."[5] Esperanza Vélez cooks because she loves it. "Clases de cocina nunca tomé. Lo que pasa es que a mí me gusta guisar. A mí sí me gusta guisar" (Cooking class, I never took. What happens is that I like to cook. I do like to cook). The assertiveness in talking about or making something she is quite capable of doing well lets her describe the procedure of cooking beans in a matter-of-fact tone, asserting her sensory knowledge.

> I put my beans on the stove; I only put a bit of oil, a piece of onion, and enough water. Enough water so when the beans are cooking you won't need to add any more, at all! Be-cause the trick is that the water you added at the beginning be enough for the beans to cook.

Therefore, I add the right amount of water, and I cover them, and then just leave them
there. When they are cooked, I check them one more time. When they are almost cooked,
I take my salt and I add it to the beans making the sign of the cross. I taste them, if they
need more salt, another cross. I taste them again, and let them cook for just a little bit
longer, and I turn the stove off. You eat a plate of frijoles de la olla *and they would*
taste wonderful. And if you cook them in the pressure cooker, they don't have the same
flavor.[6]

Esperanza Vélez's knowledge is indicative of someone who believes in her
sazón. The *sazón* here captures the notion of *saber* rather than *conocer*. *Saber* is at
an epistemological level while *conocer* relates more to the technical operation
of cooking. These two concepts are not mutually exclusive, and Esperanza
Vélez's cooking involves both.

Whether the *sazón* is a *don* (a divine gift) and whether the meals prepared
by those who have it are considered healthy or not, having a *sazón* certainly
involves an acute awareness of a sensory epistemology. The *sazón* captures the
finesse, the nuances, the flair of something that involves a specific chemistry
between the relationship of food, its preparation, and the person preparing it,
a relationship that leads to philosophical everyday observations. Within the
context of Mexican women, the efforts to define the *sazón* carry a long history.
As a way of illustrating this, I offer the most prevalent and relevant example.
Sor Juana Inés de la Cruz, a seventeenth-century Mexican nun known nowadays in Mexico as the intellectual mother of Mexican women, places the kitchen
and cooking as a discursive "sitio y lengua" (space and language) for women's
knowledge, especially in a society, like hers, that denied women the right to
university studies. She indicates that within the often-mundane practices of
cooking, a woman's labor, lies a wealth of knowledge: cooking offers lessons in
chemistry, physics, and philosophy.

Well, and what then shall I tell you . . . of the secrets of nature that I have learned while
cooking? I observe that an egg becomes solid and cooks in butter or oil, and on the con-
trary that it dissolves in sugar syrup. Or again, to ensure that sugar flows freely one
need only add the slightest bit of water that has held quince or some other sour fruit.
The yolk and white of the very same egg are of such a contrary nature that when eggs
are used with sugar, each part separately may be used perfectly well, yet they cannot be
mixed together. I shall not weary you with such inanities, which I relate simply to give
you a full account of my nature, and I believe this will make you laugh. But in truth . . .
what can we women know, save philosophies of the kitchen? It was well put by Lupericio
Leonardo [sic] that one can philosophize quite well while preparing supper. I often say,
when I make these little observations, "Had Aristotle cooked, he would have written a
great deal more."[7]

Sor Juana uses the kitchen and the practices of cooking as one of her many
tactics to "unmask the semantics of repression" toward women's knowledge.[8]

Most of the references I have read about Sor Juana's expression of kitchen
philosophy in connection to women's knowledge do not mention that
Sor Juana employs the kitchen and cooking rhetorically. I underscore this

observation neither as a criticism of Sor Juana's quintessential work, which does unveil different ecclesiastic and civil layers of repression against women's intellectual freedom, nor to suggest that Sor Juana did not cook, but to illustrate how in Sor Juana's discursive kitchen space the sense of sight dominates over the other senses. The first obvious reason for the omission of the rest of the *sazón*'s senses is that, unlike the *living* kitchen of the *charlas*, Sor Juana's kitchen is a *rhetorical* space she writes about in *La Respuesta* (1691). Perhaps a less obvious reason is Sor Juana's goal: the right to pursue an intellectual life within the world of science and literature, which she felt was *her* calling. This is a form of knowledge perceived, understood, and conceptualized, for the most part, through the sense of vision. Sor Juana's observation of culinary knowledge, just like Esperanza Vélez's reason for evoking God when she adds salt to her food, also expresses an aspect of Sor Juana's own life story: Her personal quest for a textually based intellectual life. The difference between a *rhetorical* and *living* kitchen lies in the kind of sensory knowledge used to operate within such space. Neither Sor Juana nor I define the kitchen as women's proper place of knowledge. The *sazón* involved in the living kitchen simultaneously uses all senses. The argument here illustrates how the knowledge that exists in the process of cooking all too often gets ignored as irrelevant.

THE HISTORICAL DIVISION OF THE SENSES

The significant academic attention foodways presently enjoys in the social sciences and humanities is not prevalent in the area of philosophy. Two reasons account for the absence of philosophical studies on foodways. First, food and cooking challenge notions of objectivity due to their continuously varying nature. Food and cooking habits change constantly within cultures, regions, and families. Second, the responsibility for preparing most meals historically has been the work of women, slaves, or labor workers. In part, these two social issues presumably render food and cooking philosophically insignificant and unreliable for developing theories applicable to all, at all times. These notions reflect the dualism between mind (the objective) and body (the subjective). The separation of mind and body, deemed necessary to achieve knowledge, raises a problematic question, as philosopher Lisa M. Heldke points out: "how can we *knowers* ever know anything which is *that* separate/different from us?"[9] Some philosophers, like Lisa M. Heldke, Deane W. Curtin, and Carolyn Korsmeyer, speculate that if cooking had received more attention from the time philosophies about human nature were beginning to develop, the distinction between theory (mind) and practices (body) might not have taken root. Philosophy, as "a culturally located critique of widely held beliefs using resources, methods, and attitudes present in the culture," argues philosopher Scott L. Pratt, should include as philosophical activities storytelling, ceremonies, treatise-writing, practices accessible to most. Philosophy, states Pratt, is not something only for an elite class of specialist.[10]

The chapter's opening dialogue between Vásquez, Villicaña, and me raises the issue of the senses' ability to transform sensations into forms of knowledge. It also illustrates how Western philosophy, unconsciously perhaps, influences Vásquez and me. Vásquez places her sensory knowledge on *la mano*, her touch, even without having a language to explain such practice. Yet my own inclination privileges sight, as I suggested to Vásquez that she calculates the amount of water when cooking rice by seeing its level in the pan. Our emphasis on different senses as the sources of knowledge reflects the compartmentalization Western thought gives to the senses according to their epistemological faculties.

Anthropologist Paul Stoller in *The Taste of Ethnographic Things* (1989), a study that examines the vital role senses other than vision play in the lives of the Songhay of Niger, offers an explanation for Vásquez's preference for touch as the sense of knowledge and my own quick preference for sight. Hegel, states Stoller, created the lead in "separating the intelligible from the sensible" senses. The "intelligible" incorporates only the senses of vision and hearing, known as the "higher senses"; the "lower senses," by contrast, are taste, smell, and touch. The fundamental distinction is that the "higher senses" are conceived of as objective, whereas the "lower senses" are subjective.[11] The different senses Vásquez and I favored, within Hegel's theory, place touch at the lower level of knowledge and sight at the highest. My suggestion here is not that Vásquez's knowledge is sense-driven and mine logic-driven. Using my own experience, I hope to prove this assumption not to be the case by demonstrating how Western thought influences our relationship to the senses. My academic training leads me to select the sense of sight; Vásquez's culinary experiences lead her to ground her knowledge on a bodily sense.

From the beginning of Western philosophy, the senses were divided in terms of higher and lower, separating sight and hearing as those which contribute to the "highest achievement of human efforts: knowledge, morals, and art."[12] Within these two, sight, for Aristotle, came first. In his words, "All men by nature desire to know. An indication of this is the delight we take in our senses; for even apart from their usefulness they are loved for themselves; and above all others the sense of sight . . . The reason is that this, most of all the senses, makes us know and brings to light many differences between things."[13] Sight and hearing are distal senses that operate by perceiving and processing world experiences directed outward, away from the immediate body. Seemingly, the detachment from the immediate body makes them sources of objective information, for one can see or hear something "without entering into a relationship with it."[14] With the emergence of scientific culture, the idea of personal detachment in order to gain objective information was further advanced by the emphasis on empirical knowledge. Empirical knowledge, says Stoller, "raised sight to a privileged position," neglecting the other sensory-logic, particularly, touch, taste, and smell."[15] Nietzsche expresses a similar concern as he argues, "Over the course of history, the visual has increasingly taken precedence over elements of thought and action deriving from the other senses (the faculty of hearing and the act of listening, for instance, or the hand and the voluntary acts of 'grasping,' 'holding,' and so on)."[16] Nietzsche goes on to say that the privilege of sight extends to the point "that the senses of smell, taste, and touch have almost completely [been] annexed and absorbed by sight."[17] The consequence of these philosophical views places sight and hearing as the only senses necessary for forming rational, reflective, and theoretical concepts, fundamental in the development of universal truths.

The lower senses—touch, taste, and smell—in contrast to the higher senses, perceive and process world experience in the body. The fact that they are bodily senses renders information gained through them subjective because such sensations vary from person to person. In addition, the senses of taste and smell are considered "primitive." Carolyn Korsmeyer attributes this view to the fact that these senses "evolved for protective purposes necessary for life and to some extent still function that way." While this is true, Korsmeyer points out the negative implications in conceptualizing some senses as "primitive." For one thing, it suggests that they have not progressed beyond their early stages. Also, since they function in a similar manner in lower life forms as in humans, "they are unworthy of extended" philosophical attention. "The danger of the term 'primitive' when applied to taste and smell," argues Korsmeyer, "is that it is very easy to slide from the sense of 'early,' 'basic,' to the sense of 'uncivilized.'" When this takes place, Korsmeyer suggests, "we are back in the territory of the theorists who classify the bodily senses as less worthy than the higher ones on moral grounds."[18] Overindulgence in the bodily senses, closely connected to the desire and pleasure of food, drink, and sex, creates the immorality of the lower senses, for they distract an individual from the path's journey to universal truths. Everything associated with bodily desires that might clutter reason requires control. Consequently, within this dualistic aspect of Western thought, the lower senses connected with the body are easily dismissed as lacking credibility and as not providing empirical forms of knowledge. They are, in the words of Suzanne Langer, "reason's disgrace."[19]

The argument that the so-called lower senses—smell, touch, and taste—have no epistemological value only devalues people's corporeal ways of knowing. Yet this has not always been the case. In *Aroma: The Cultural History of Smell*, Constance Classen, David Howes, and Anthony Synnott (1994) explain that in the premodern West, smell held a different epistemological status that actually challenges modern linear worldview. They explain that "odour was thought of as [an] intrinsic 'essence' revelatory of inner truth. Through smell, therefore, one interacted with interiors, rather than with surfaces, as one did through sight. Furthermore, odours cannot be readily contained; they escape and cross boundaries, blending different entities into olfactory wholes. Such a sensory model can be seen to be opposed to our modern, linear worldview."[20] Since smell and taste are essential in conceptualizing the structures of some societies by taking an outer reality and experiencing it in the body, these senses have been "marginalized because it is felt that [they] threaten the abstract and impersonal regime of modernity by virtue of [their] radical inferiority, [their] boundary-transgressing properties and [their] emotional potency."[21] Stoller, in *Embodying Colonial Memories* (1995), echoes this same argument.[22] The marginalization of the bodily senses dates to the late eighteenth century and early nineteenth century when philosophers and scientists decided that "sight was the preeminent sense of reason and civilization, [and] smell was the sense of madness and savagery."[23] Furthermore, the sense of smell in the nineteenth century became feminized, as it was associated with intuition, sentiment, homemaking, and seduction. The division of the senses, therefore, relates to the philosophical split between thought and practice, the eternal and the temporal, the universal and the particular, the mind and the body, that which is masculine and that which is feminine. As a matter of fact, an implicit gendering separates the senses: "the ability to transcend the body to govern the senses, to gain knowledge, is a masculine ability that when exercised well will keep one embodied as a male. [T]herefore, . . . the higher, distal sense of sight and hearing paired up with the controlling intellect of a virtuous man, and the lower, proximal senses [paired up] with the appetites and the dangerous pleasures that are in one way or another associated with femininity."[24] Such separation is purely philosophical because the faculty of the senses operates the same way in both men and women. What this indicates, however, is a "split between some rather vague concept of femininity associated with the bodily senses and actual females, a split that is responsible for a great deal of incoherence in conceptual frameworks where gender lurks."[25]

Elizabeth Grosz argues that the source of the "crisis of reason" experienced in the twentieth century "is in part a consequence of the historical privileging of the purely conceptual or mental over the corporeal."[26] Even with the basic fundamental differences between the senses, as shown above, sight and hearing projecting reality outside the body and the other senses taking an outer reality into the body, all the senses are connected to a subjective and emotional person. The *sazón* highlights the conceptual difficulty of the seeming necessity to separate mind and body in the quest of knowledge.[27] In the realm of food and cooking, the *sazón's* sensory epistemology shows the interconnection of all the senses as cognitive devices. Since food is experienced through all the senses and taken into the body, it rejects the separation of mind and body. Developing spaces for a sensory-logic, for the logic of the *sazón*, alleviates the "crisis of reason" and shows how the "lower senses" are not "reason's disgrace" because the body is a source of cognitive and intuitive knowledge. Stoller suggests that such spaces, within the field of ethnography, are found when researchers do not make the Eurocentric mistake of believing that sight is the only orientation in conceptualizing the world. In some cultures "the senses of taste or smell are more important than vision."[28] A sensory-logic demonstrates that sight and hearing achieved their higher status due to political and economic power and not to their capacity for objective, disembodied epistemologies.[29]

FOOD'S SOCIAL AND SCIENTIFIC CONCEPTUAL KNOWLEDGE

The *sazón* is a corporeal, sensual knowledge. Yet to understand its epistemology, we must first find ways of gaining back the body as a center of knowledge. The *sazón's* sensory-logic, inseparable from food, thus inseparable from the body, values the ordinary, as the activity of cooking and eating, which in turn leads to regain a sense of ourselves as cognitive bodily creatures. If one way the mind controls the body is through the denial of food, which extends to the denial of corporeal knowledge, in embracing food as central to the development of philosophies, the body becomes a source of knowledge.[30] Since food is the "most common and pervasive source of human experience," food as a source of knowledge goes beyond an individual's likes and dislikes.[31] To understand the *sazón*'s corporeal knowledge, philosopher Michel de Certeau's concept of a "science of singularities" is useful since it studies the relationship of everyday practices to particular circumstances, and the local networks that are constantly affected by social-economic constraints.[32] We can say, then, that the corporeal knowledge involved in the practice of everyday cooking offers a way of thinking about food, as philosopher Uma Narayan says, that "can help reveal the rich and messy textures of our attempts at self-understanding, as well as our interesting and problematic understanding of our relationship" to and with others.[33] These are relationships experienced in the body.

In *Food, the Body, and the Self* (1996), Deborah Lupton theorizes about the interaction among food, embodiment, and subjectivity. Lupton argues that this interaction combines cognitive discourses and "non or pre-discursive sensual and embodied experiences [by which] individuals come to understand themselves, their bodies, and their relationships to the food they are eating. Touch, taste, smell, hearing, and sight are our entrées into culture. Food, of course, has a supremely physical presence, and we interact with this presence through our senses: we smell, taste, see, and touch food, and sometimes hear it (for example, the sizzling of frying food). We do not necessarily need language and discourse to experience food. However, language and discourse are integral to the meanings we construct around food—how we interpret and convey to others our sensual experiences in preparing, touching, and eating food—which in turn shape our sensual responses."[34] Sensual responses, a combination of cognitive and embodied experiences, inform philosophies that come out from people's specific cultural and historical realities. The grassroots theorists from the *charlas* place food and sensory logic, the *sazón*, at the center of culinary knowledge, calling into question how much the so-called lower senses have in fact been annexed and absorbed by sight, as Nietzsche suggests.

Hilaria Cortés, in a brief moment of our *charlas*, indicates that perhaps sight only absorbs the other senses when a person does not have, as she says, "la costumbre" of using and valuing all the senses as sources of knowledge. When Cortés and I broached the topic of cookbooks and recipes that call for exact measurements and procedures, first Cortés admits to not owning any cookbooks, then she says, "It depends on people's custom. Here, Americans are more civilized people; it's the correct way, right? The measurement. But when you don't have time to measure or when you don't have the curiosity to measure, it doesn't matter. Because you have the measurement in the feel of your hands and in your precision of vision. All you need is your eyes and your hands. But if you don't have the right feeling in your hand, or the right sense of vision, well then you will need to measure. But if you have such [forms] of calculating [with your hand and eyes], you don't need measuring utensils."[35] Cortés's comments question the validity of adhering to just one form of epistemological understanding.

Cortés acknowledges that cooking with scientific precision involves money and time. To cook with scientific precision, women are expected to employ every machine, device, or apparatus as these become items of *necessity*. The concept of time, feminist geographer Massey reminds us, "is aligned with history, progress, civilization, politics, transcendence, and [thus] coded masculine. And it is the opposite of these things which have ... been coded feminine."[36] Cortés echoes this association in terms of nationalities as she connects the measuring utensil with the correct civilized form employed by American people. The marketing strategies of consumption, the ideologies of first world superiority (Americans) over third world inferiority (Mexicans), control scientific culinary methodologies and not the sense of sight in and of itself.

Scientific discourse, with its precise culinary measurements that rely on the sense of sight, aims to legitimize itself as the only efficient culinary practice, thus eliminating the *sazón*'s sensory-logic, based on all of the senses. Cortés's comment indicates the fallacy of such an assumption by placing in a parallel continuum both sight (*el ojo*) and touch (*la mano*) as forms of sensory epistemology. Cortés bases this form of knowledge in "la costumbre," a continuous participation in the culture of the senses. For Cortés, one only needs measuring utensils if one does not have *el tantéo* (the calculation of the hand); thus she provides a distinction between the efficiency of material utensils and dexterity. If a person lacks understanding of the epistemology of all the senses, then such a person must depend on material apparatus. Cortés emphasizes culinary methods and procedures that differ according to culture and class. This correlation of all the senses is found throughout the *charlas*.

The *sazón* relies on an interconnection of all the senses, sight always included but not necessary privileged. The grassroots theorists from the *charlas* do what some contemporary academics suggest the study of food and cooking illustrates: the inseparability of the senses and their collective cognitive function. Yet some academics, including me, continue to draw a separation due to our tendency for binary thinking despite our best intentions to do otherwise. For example, in the first *charla* with Vélez, once again it was I who privileged sight over the other senses. As she describes the process for making masa for tortillas she says:

> To let the ears of corn became maize, you don't cut them from the plant. Leave them there until they turn yellow, until the leaves are dry. Then you can cut them. Then you remove the grains from the cob, and you make the corn dough. You cook the grains in water to which you add some unslaked lime. But you have to know how much unslaked lime to add; you need to know how strong it should be . . . because if you add too much lime, the masa would turn out yellow, and it would taste bad. Therefore, you have to know how much unslaked lime to add to the water. And you also have to know what is the right degree of cooking. To know if the grains of corn are cooked, take one and if its shin comes off, then it's done. Then you take it off the stove. You leave it sitting in the water until the next day. The next day, you drain it and grind it.[37]

Since Vélez mentions the importance of knowing exactly how much unslaked lime one must add to the water when soaking corn to make masa, I asked her how I would know the *quantity*, empirical means of knowledge, of unslaked lime to add. She looked at me with an expression that made me feel I had asked a rather obvious question. She did answer my question. Extending one of her hands, she showed me her palm while with the other she made a gesture as if gathering unslaked lime out of a sack and pouring it into her open palm and said: "te la pones así, la sientes pa' calcular" (you put it in like this; you feel it in order to calculate). Vélez's culinary knowledge goes beyond touch as the necessary sense for making masa. Not only "la mano" determines the amount of lime but also smell. Touch, to weigh the unslaked lime, and smell, to determine the right potency, correspond in importance with the sense of taste and sight. Too much lime and the tortillas turn out yellow, and they taste bad.

Contreras not only affirms the equality of the senses, but she also questions my own insistence in determining quantities by a process of using measuring utensils. While giving me a list of "add this and add that" to a boiling pot in the process of making *pozole*, I stopped her and asked for quantities:

> **Meredith:** *And quantities, how do you know? You say, "I put this and I add that." But how much? Portions. How do you know?*

> **Alma:** *I don't know about quantities because that is something I just calculate.*

> **Meredith:** *How do you calculate? How do you know?*

> **Alma:** *Well, depending on how much I am making. Onion. I use a whole onion if I am making a big pot. I add salt, and that is determined by taste. Everyone can determine the amount of salt according to their taste. Some people like food more salty than others do. Chile. Normally one bag. If I want it very spicy, two bags.*[38]

Once again, as with other women in the *charlas*, for Contreras cooking by calculation does not mean just touch but an integration of different senses. As the women from the *charlas* describe their culinary practices, it is evident that they have not forgotten the importance of the so-called lower senses.

The *sazón's* cognitive sensory-logic involves foods' chemical reactions learned from many years of experimenting in the kitchen. After Contreras shares her two ways of making American or Mexican beans, she says that for beans not to turn brown, if they need water while cooking, the water must be hot. Hilaria Cortés, Liduvina Vélez, Guadalupe Flores, Alicia Villanueva, and Esperanza Vélez confirm this process when we broach the topic of cooking beans. Throughout the *charlas* there are numerous examples revealing a sophisticated awareness of food's chemistry. María Luisa Cárdenas learned from her mother, who would grow her own vegetables, that in the process of preparing cabbage for tostadas one must chop it early in the day and add baking soda. According to Cárdenas's mother, this was "para materle los animalitos" (to kill all the insects it might have). We have already seen some chemical culinary understanding in Liduvina Vélez's knowledge of adding unslaked lime to water for soaking maize.

Esperanza Vélez expresses a similar knowledge when she gives me a recipe for making *pipián verde* (pumpkin-seed sauce). When making this sauce, she says that one must add enough oil to the frying pan and add salt to the pan, "para que no te brinquen tanto porque es un brincadero tremendo" (so that the seeds do not scatter all over the place). One must know to what degree the seeds must be fried; if they over fry "se te amargan" (they taste bitter).

> *Meredith:* [If you over fry them], do they taste bitter like garlic does?

> *Esperanza:* Correct, the seeds have the same reaction as garlic. If they are over fried, they will taste bitter; they will burn, and the seed will have a different color and a different taste. It does not require much (time or ingredients] to prepare pipián and it is so good. Whenever I have to visit someone and bring a dish, people say, "Oh, señora you have to bring the pipián verde." "Esperanza, you have to bring the pipián verde?" Why? Because everyone loves [my] pipián verde.

> *Meredith:* Have you eaten other people's pipián?

> *Esperanza:* Yes.

> *Meredith:* And does it come out different?

> *Esperanza:* Well, it is not the same thing.[39]

Perhaps one reason many people like and request Esperanza Vélez's *pipián verde* is because she knows yet another chemical reaction involved in preparing it. She explains that this sauce separates if the hands of different people get involved in the process of cooking it. In Vélez's words, "Es que es un guisado muy especial que no permite que otra gente le meta mano" (It's a special dish that does not let other people stick their hands in). Erika Morales shared a similar observation when we discussed the process of making *barbacoa Veracruzana*. A key ingredient for this Veracruz-style barbecue, made either with beef, pork, or chicken, is a leaf called "acuyo." *Acuyo* comes from a tropical tree native of the region of Veracruz, similar in taste to avocado leaves. Morales says that "no más no debe de pasar [el punto de cocerse] de la hoja porque es muy hostigoza" (you must know the right amount of time to cook the leaf because if overcooked it tastes cloying).

Why does adding salt to a frying pan prevent the squash seeds from bursting out of the pan? Why does the *pipián* sauce separate if someone other than the cook stirs it? Why does overcooking *acuyo* make it taste *hostigozo*? Why when cooking *maíz* to make masa, as Liduvina Vélez mentions above, is it necessary to know the right ratio of unslaked lime and water to soak *maíz*? None of the women from the *charlas* gave me a specific scientific explanation for these chemical reactions. But nowadays, in the case of soaking *maíz* with unslaked lime when preparing it for making masa for tortillas, scientific research proves that this process of dissolving unslaked lime in water increases "the calcium content to at least twenty times that in the original maize while possibly increasing the availability of certain amino acids."[40] The tortilla eaters of Mesoamerica have been the only group of people to use *maíz* as their main item of diet who have not suffered from the plague of pellagra. Arnold J. Bauer explains that "among dedicated corn eaters the sole exception to the plague of pellagra were the people of Meso-America and the humble tortilla claims substantial credit. Maize is low in pellagra-preventing niacin and, moreover, what is present exists in a chemically bound form. The addition of lime, however, frees the bound niacin so there is some evidence for the beneficial effect of this treatment. More important was the practice of eating tortillas in conjunction with beans and chiles, which provide protection against pellagra."[41]

Bauer is not convinced that the pre-Columbian people were consciously adding lime for nutritional reasons for *maíz*. Liduvina Vélez, like millions of peasant people throughout the years, however, without conducting laboratory studies and without the scientific discourse of pellagra-preventing niacin, guided by her sensory-logic developed a fairly well balanced diet gathered from both *la costumbre*, a sensory culture, and her limited local resources.

The *sazón*'s cognitive aspects also involve a social dimension. Multiculturalism, for instance, according to food historian Donna Gabaccia, in *We Are What We Eat: Ethnic Food and the Making of Americans* (1998), is something we experience *in* our bodies by the foods we are willing to eat. Gabaccia states that for Americans "multicultural is not so much its many separate culinary traditions as it is Americans' desire to eat a multi-ethnic mix of foods, and to make this mix part of themselves."[42] In this case, the experience of multicultural politics takes place *in* the body. In the *charlas*, something similar takes place when women define aspects of their cooking practices in terms of ethnic or national politics. A number of women from the *charlas* express some effects of this form of multiculturalism in their process of cooking and the intake of such foods. For instance, Contreras expresses two forms of cooking beans as Mexican and American; their distinction is not only in terms of color but also in how much time it takes to cook them. Contreras prepares either "güeritos" (white) beans or "prietitos" (brown) beans by simply altering the cooking method.

> *Alma: I never measure the water. But the recipe so that beans don't turn out brown is that once they begin to boil you must turn the heat down and cover them. Slowly they cook by themselves; I don't add more water. Therefore, they take longer to cook, but they come out white. Therefore, when I feel like having American beans, I do them this way. When I feel like having Mexican beans, I do them fast. I keep adding and adding water so that they cook fast and they come out brown.*

> *Meredith: But why some American and some Mexican?*

> *Alma: The Americans are white and the Mexicans are brown.... Therefore, it depends on how much time you have [to cook them].*[43]

In the process of cooking beans, Contreras differentiates between American (white) beans and Mexican (brown) beans. American beans, "güeritos," are associated with a certain amount of excess time. Mexican beans, "prietos," are associated with a lifestyle "on-the-run." The pigmentation of beans and this supposed representation of national identities reflects a racial stereotype. Contreras, as a Mexican woman living in the United States, however, does not adhere to the divisiveness of the stereotype. In her description of cooking beans, Contreras does not select one over the other. She cooks beans using both procedures, and she eats them both, a culinary symbolic acceptance of both cultures. Her cooking habits are not traditional in the sense that she eats Mexican food. As a matter of fact, while she has a habit of eating out a lot, she rarely goes to Mexican restaurants. She prefers to go, as she says, "a la comida china, las pastas, las ensaladas" (Chinese food, pastas, salads). But she also has a genuine appetite for "enchiladas, pozole, albóndigas, and sopitos."

Cortés speaks of yet another way of how through her cooking process she appropriates the food of "los americanos" (the Americans) and makes it "comida de la raza mexicana" (food of Mexican people). This dialogue takes place as I asked her about the time she used to sell hot dogs.

> **Meredith:** *Tell me, how did you do selling hot dogs?*
>
> **Yaya:** *Sometimes good, sometimes bad. Well, selling hot dogs you can make some good money if you find the right place to sell. If you find a good place where there are Hispanics, but mainly Mexicans because if they are Salvadoran, you won't sell hot dogs.*
>
> **Meredith:** *Why do you think that's the case?*
>
> **Yaya:** *Because Salvadorans only buy traditional things from their country. Pupusas, fried bananas with beans. All those things. You can't sell hot dogs to them. But if there are Mexicans, hot dogs sell well.*
>
> **Meredith:** *But why if hot dogs are not our own food?*
>
> **Yaya:** *No but they are "perros calientes" of our country. Just change the name from hot dogs to "perros calientes" of our country. . . . Before, I used to sell a lot of hot dogs. Now, I have not sold them for a long time. Since I now live in a new place, and there are mainly Salvadorans where I live.*[44]

The inversion of "hot dogs" to "perros calientes" takes away the symbolic American association of this food, making it Mexican, especially since they are cooked with a strip of bacon around them, grilled onions, and a salsa of cooked tomatoes, onion, and *serrano chiles* instead of ketchup. Here, Cortés also indicates that multiculturalism's ability to enter our bodies has its limits; Salvadorans from her neighborhood in Los Angeles are not as open to accepting "perros calientes" as Mexicans are. Food's social conception is one that every chapter of *Voices* explores in different forms.

The *sazón's* sensory-logic is not constrained to an unchanging methodological or conceptual paradigm. Contreras stresses the particularities and subjective elements of sensory knowledge as she says "cualquiera puede calcular al gusto" (anyone can calculate to their taste). The social meaning of the *sazón* changes *al gusto* (to the taste of each person). By acknowledging people's own understanding of *al gusto*, Contreras admits that sensory knowledge *is* subjective and a matter of perspective. Using *al gusto* as a feminist culinary theoretical concept, we can clearly illustrate that knowledge is always subjective and not based on a separation between the mental and the physical. Elizabeth Grosz argues that "to admit that knowledges are but perspectives—points of view on the world—is to acknowledge that other, quite different positions and perspectives are possible." Grosz goes on to say that one must accept the diverse series of influences, "some rational, some not, some universal, some highly particularized" in the production and nature of knowledge.[45] The *sazón* as a corporal knowledge is not an inversion of the senses' higher/lower status. What most of the grassroots theorists from the *charlas* change is the senses' hierarchical, vertical paradigm into a concept that places all five senses in horizontal parallel lines.

The grassroots theorists' concept of *al gusto* resonates with postmodern and poststructuralist discourses of subjectivity. Generally speaking, postmodernism inclines "toward the unstable, fluid, fragmented, indeterminate, . . . for that which resists definition, closure, and fixity."[46] Likewise, poststructuralist theory examines the social construction of the nature of knowledge. It emphasizes the centrality of language in understanding social interactions without forgetting the fluidity in the meaning of language as a source of communication. Poststructuralists influenced by postmodernism provide a theoretical lens to see that our identity is not a unified self but rather a multitude of fragments that make up our subjectivity. The term subjectivity describes "the manifold ways in which individuals understand themselves in relation to others and experience their lives. Subjectivity is a less rigid term than identity, as it incorporates the understanding that the self, or more accurately, selves, are highly chargeable and contextual, albeit within certain limits imposed by the culture in which an individual lives, including power relations, social institutions and hegemonic discourses."[47] *Al gusto* suggests this particular concept of subjectivity, since food habits reflect much about our sense of self. When the women from the *charlas* say that *al gusto* one adds salt, chile, onion, garlic to one's cooking, they speak of people's notion of a fluid sense of self using terms of the *sazón's* sensual-logic of subjectivity.

The *al gusto* embedded in the *sazón* is where individuals' life stories are revealed. The *sazón* with its *al gusto* subjective, corporal intrinsic logic leads to investigations of "life stories of individuals as opposed to totalizing investigations."[48] Such type of investigation enables us to understand how individuals are able to assert agency even when their lives faced social, economic, or gender challenges. The *sazón's* element of *al gusto*, using Luce Giard's words, can be defined as how each woman creates "her own style according to how she accents a certain element of a [cooking] practice, [of] how she applies herself to one or another [method of cooking, of] how she creates her personal way of navigating through [already] accepted, allowed, and ready-made [cooking] techniques."[49] To this list of defining a woman's *sazón*, I add invention, or piecing together, of new cross-cultural and geo-social culinary techniques. In this newness, subversion to establish social "norms" takes place.

During the *charlas*, for example, all the women speak of the implications of modernization and how technology can, does, and must alter cultural and traditional practices. In the *charlas*, Mexican traditions and cultural practices can be spoken of as culture-in-transition. One reference to this transition is the use of microwaves or toaster ovens in order to expedite Contreras's own process of making enchiladas. As Contreras explains her process of making enchiladas, she indicates how many people, in order to sit down and eat together, normally would make a lot of enchiladas and put them in the oven. Later they put everything on the table and they eat. Contreras, however, does not like them this way.

> *Duvi: Well, it is more work to be making them as people are eating. But they taste better; their steamy flavor.*

> *Meredith: But with the other way, everybody can sit together.*

> *Alma: Yes, but I don't like them that way. I like the enchiladas to be almost crisp. Not soggy.*

> *Meredith: And when do you eat?*

> *Duvi: At the end.*

> *Alma: At the end. When everyone is done, I prepare mine. Or I try to make them fast so that there might still be one person eating who would eat with me.*

> *Duvi: And in the micro, mi'ja. Maybe in the micro it would work.*

> *Alma: No, where it would work very well is in those little toaster ovens. Maybe in those ovens, it might work because they would be the same. I have heated tamales in the little toaster ovens and they are good. Better than if you use the microwave.*[50]

In this segment of our *charla*, both Liduvina Vélez and Alma Contreras believe in a certain methodological process of making enchiladas to achieve a perfect *al gusto* taste, texture, and flavor that is characteristic of Contreras's own *sazón*. This moment of our *charla* shows how the interconnection of some modern techniques in the process of making enchiladas does not significantly alter Contreras's own *al gusto* style of enchiladas, known in my house as "las famosas enchiladas de Alma" (Alma's famous enchiladas).

Another dish discussed in a number of *charlas* that indicates personal stories as people add their own *al gusto* are *chilaquiles*. *Chilaquiles* is a rather simple meal, nothing more than fried tortillas, salsa, cheese, cream, and, if they are to be authentic, one must add a few leaves of epazote. Although *chilaquiles* are simple to make, it is not simple to make them with *sazón*. Verónica Abarca, my sister-in-law, for instance, tells me that although her mother makes wonderful *chilaquiles*, she herself cannot: "Mi mamá hace los chilaquiles ¡deliciosos! Nó, nó, yo nó sé hacer chilaquiles. Nó sé por qué, pero nó me salen" (My mother makes delicious *chilaquiles*. No, I don't know how to make them. When I make them they don't turn out well). Abarca explains her mother's procedure in making *chilaquiles*; therefore, her inability to make them is not based on not understanding culinary technicalities. In her case, the lack of her *sazón*, as she explains in our *charla*, is perhaps based on her own disinterest in the discipline of culinary studies, a discipline where her own mother finds much pleasure. Abarca says, "Well, cooking is something that my mother enjoys. Something that I don't enjoy. Well, when I lived at home, she would tell me, 'come and see so that you can cook when you get married.' I hated the kitchen. I have never, never liked to cook."[51]

When Vélez speaks of her own *chilaquiles*, she says that "la gracia de los chilaquiles es que te queden las tortillas doraditas, pero no fritas" (the trick of the *chilaquiles* is in frying the tortillas to the right degree). Vélez's *sazón* for *chilaquiles* is not obtained by following a prescriptive culinary method; after all, Vélez claims that everyone has their own style of making *chilaquiles*, their own *al gusto*. In the particular case of Vélez's *chilaquiles*, her *sazón* captures and articulates the sense of her working-class roots. Vélez always categorizes her *chilaquiles* as "la comida de uno de pobre" (the food of we the poor). When I taste the *sazón* in "los chilaquiles de mi 'amá," I am always reminded of her intelligence, ingenuity, and, most of all, her courage, all of which she reveals in her *sazón* as she cooks *la comida de uno de pobre*. The trajectory of Vélez's culinary knowledge and her personal use of it demonstrate the acts of agency embedded on the *sazón*. In my own making of *chilaquiles*, my *sazón* serves as a savory expression of my feelings toward my adopted families, the only ones with the reserved privilege to enjoy my *chilaquiles* as they are an integral part of my life. Each person's *sazón*, therefore, carries personal, cultural, and social messages that exceed the preparation of a meal.

The *sazón's* sensory-logic manifests itself through bodily techniques. The *charlas* demonstrate how "doing-cooking," Luce Giard's words, is in fact as much a mental activity as it is a manual labor. Giard defines the activity of doing-cooking as one that requires intelligence, imagination, and a twofold memorization: one of gestures and the other of senses. A study of women's process of doing-cooking, as we have seen, and will continue to see throughout *Voices*, leads to a study of women's "subtle intelligence which is full of nuances and strokes of genius."[52] Understanding such intelligence involves an awareness of the memory process necessary for a culinary production. Giard categorizes memory into three distinctive processes: apprenticeship, programming, and sensory perception. Memory of apprenticeship refers to "the witness of gestures"; a programming memory operates the astute calculation of both preparation and cooking time, and a memory of sensory perception is more important "than the theoretical cooking time indicated in the recipe; it is the smell coming from the oven that lets one know if the cooking is coming along" as it should be.[53] The memory of apprenticeship requires the performance of two specific culinary gestures, technical and expressive, which involve the "movement[s] of the body as well as the mind." Technical gestures are "inhabited by a necessity (material or symbolic), a meaning and a belief." Whether a technical gesture requires a tool, as a knife, or only the bare hands, it "calls for an entire mobilization of the body"; therefore, it is a body technique. The technical gesture expresses "invention, tradition, and education to give [gestures] a form of efficacy that suits the physical makeup and practical intelligence of the person who uses [them]."[54] Of expressive gestures, Giard simply says that they "translate a feeling or a reaction."[55]

In the *charlas*, both technical and expressive gestures are inseparable. A number of women mentioned the *metate* and the *mano*, a sort of mortar and pestle, used to grind corn as well as chiles, nuts, chocolate, and other things. The *metate* is a wide, flat rectangular surface that resembles a three-legged table with the front two legs shorter than the back leg; the *mano*, the hand, is a long semicircular stone, both usually made of basalt rock. The *metate* itself, in many households, is a symbol of familial history. Alicia Villanueva says that part of her inheritance, of the legacy her mother is leaving to her, is "el metate." Villanueva will inherit her mother's *metate* since she is the youngest daughter. Cortés, when speaking of the history of her aunt's *metate*, the one her mother has always used, says, "The *metate* my aunt has belonged to her grandmother, my great-grandmother. It's like a hundred and thirty years, or more! If my aunt is ninety, and her grandmother gave it to her. Imagine!"[56] One can only imagine the stories engraved in those two pieces of stone with the *sazón* of all the women who have used it in the course of a hundred years—or more![57]

When women in the *charlas* speak about the use of the *metate*, commonly referred to as the Mexican blender, they address how their mothers have mastered the bodily technique involved in using the *metate*. While Alicia Villanueva's mother masters the skill of the *metate-mano*, her own leaves much to be desired: "My mom . . . knows how to make a very good red sauce. She grinds everything using the *metate*. When all of us went in 1990, I tried to help her. She made *mole* for all of us. I tried to help her grind. I saw how easily she would grind using the *metate*. I told her, 'let me help you, *amacita*.' I was not able to grind anything! The chile kept coming out whole. I would put pressure on it and move the *mano* of the *metate* in different ways, and the chile would remain whole. When she did it, everything would be finely ground."[58] As Villanueva remembers her mother's ability to make the chile into powder, she brings one of her hands toward her mouth making a sound with her lips as if giving a kiss, and says, "de acordarme qué rico le sale el mole" (just to remember how delicious her *mole* is).

Irma Vásquez offers an explanation that reveals the uniqueness of her own mother's technical and expressive gestures in using the *metate*—a uniqueness that explains Villanueva's own savory gesture as she remembers her mother's *sazón* for making *mole*. When Vásquez shares her mother's recipe that she likes the best, she immediately says, "Meat with chile sauce. She would fry the meat, and she would always grind chiles *guajillos* and also chile *pasilla*. She would grind them with the *metate*. I think that's what gave it its special flavor, that she would always use the *metate*. Even if she had an electric blender, she would always grind her chiles, and corn for making masa with the *metate*. I think this is what gave her *mole* its special flavor. Because otherwise, the meat with chile sauce is the same thing we make. Clean the meat, then cook the chiles. But the only difference is that we put it in the blender. She doesn't. She would always make it with the *metate*."[59] The sense of touch involved in the process of grinding spices in the *metate* reveals "the complexity of the gastrula realm [which] embraces an essentially indefinite . . . variety of codes."[60] For Vásquez and Villanueva, with each gesture of pounding the *mano* into the *metate*, their respective mothers transmit an essence of themselves into the sauces they prepare. Marcel Mauss in *The Gift* argues a similar point in relation to an economy of reciprocal gift giving. Mauss says that "to give something is to give a part of oneself . . . [O]ne gives away what is in reality a part of one's nature and substance, while to receive something is to receive a part of someone's spiritual essence."[61] When Vásquez and Villanueva eat or remember the taste of their mothers' *mole*, a part of their mothers enters their own being. The use of the body, of the hand, converts their mothers' food into soul food. The expressive gesture that transmits a feeling would get lost if instead of the *metate* and the direct use of the bare hand, Vásquez and Villanueva's mothers would use an electric blender. Vásquez and Villanueva's mothers' *sazón* and their daughters' remembrance of it is given and received through the sensual, corporeal knowledge of the *sazón*. Villanueva certainly feels strongly about this matter: "When we go, . . . she loves to make *mole* for us. And she uses the *metate*. Now she has an electric blender, and she is also getting old. But she loves to grind using the *metate*."[62]

While both Vásquez and Villanueva's mothers have electric blenders, when making *mole* for their families, they refuse to deprive themselves of their *sazón* and refuse to become what Giard calls "*unskilled spectator[s]* who watch the machine function in [their] place."[63] Giard's argument carries a tone of lamentation. She feels that modern technological instruments deny a cook the ability to use her dexterity and display her ingenuity. The connection I see between the *sazón* and bodily movement, the use of the hands without many industrial appliances, is that heavy dependency on such equipment diminishes our ability to rely on all of our senses as the guide of our culinary knowledge, a guide of social interactions and philosophical observations. Technical appliances primarily demand that we use our sense of sight and for the most part ignore the rest of the senses. The ultimate effect, therefore, is that many people begin to forget the sensory-logic and discourse of the *sazón*, which is based in the interconnection of all the senses.

One effective way of forgetting such an interconnection of all the senses is to rely too much on textually based knowledge. The more a person relies on textually based knowledge, as following directions in a cookbook requires, the more the cognitive sensory-logic of the *sazón* and confidence to cook *al gusto* gets lost. The more a person depends on cookbooks that rely on the sense of sight, the less that person grounds her/his knowledge within the epistemology of the other senses and body techniques or gestures. Contreras indicates this effect on the senses in relation to the two of us when she questions my reliance on textually based culinary knowledge. Contreras says, "I never write down measurements. You also cook only by calculating. Or do you use measurements? I don't think you go and look at the recipe. [I] don't base my cooking on a book and having to look at what must be added next in a recipe."[64] Her question to me, which suggests a suspicion regarding measuring utensils, and her answer reflect a validation of her *sazón*. Interestingly, Contreras can only re-create *al gusto* those recipes learned through her *sazón's* sensory-logic and the memory embedded in body gestures but not those recipes described and prescribed on a written text. When she recalls a carrot and orange cake that once she loved to make and made it a lot, she says:

> The ingredients. Well, you prepare flour, egg, and this thing so the cake can rise. You add carrots and orange, the skin of the orange. And you put it in the oven. And it turns out really good.

> **Meredith:** *And where did you learn this recipe?*

> **Alma:** *From a recipe in a book. But ask me to make this cake again, I don't remember how to make it that well. But I used to make it a lot.*[65]

Much culinary literature indicates that baking, unlike other forms of cooking, does require the precision of measurements. While this could explain Contreras's example, other women from the *charlas* also indicate that recipes initially learned from cookbooks can only be re-created by looking at the written text again. Yet those recipes learned through their sensory-logic remain guided by the *sazón*. On numerous occasions throughout the *charlas*, the *sazón's* corporeal knowledge remains more important than cookbooks' inscribed knowledge.[66]

Many grassroots theorists do participate in the network of sharing recipes, yet, while some of them are shared in written form, many are not. Even those recipes shared in writing often omit exact quantities. As a matter of fact, many of these women do not have an index card container filled with recipes or a collection of cookbooks. After Esperanza Vélez describes the procedures of numerous recipes that range from cooking beans, to *pipián verde, pipián rojo, chiles en nogada, pozole, tinga, el mole verde, sopas de cremas, adobado*, and so on, I asked her about the collection of recipes she has gathered throughout her lifelong practice in culinary matters.

> **Meredith:** *Tell me, all these recipes, do you have them written in a book or you know them by memory?*

> **Esperanza:** *No. I know them by memory. I don't have them written down. I know them by memory.*[67]

Like Esperanza Vélez, Liduvina Vélez, who in Mexico once sold food outside her house and later managed a restaurant where the menu changed daily, did not collect or depend on written recipes. When I ask Liduvina Vélez about written recipes she says, "Here with you is where I came to see cookbooks. Here in the houses where I'm working. And in the restaurant where I was working, the Bay Window [in California]."[68] When I asked Susana García viuda de Melo, owner of a small mini-cocina situated within the property of her home, if she had a recipe that she would call her own, one that she has invented, she addressed my question by asking her daughter to answer.

> **Meredith:** *If is okay with you, could you speak to me about your recipes?*

> **Susana:** *To speak of my recipes, yes of course.*

> **Meredith:** *Do you have a recipe that you have invented? Something that you say, "This is mine"?*[69]

García viuda de Melo smiles a little, asks me to wait and calls her daughter, Vero, and asks her to answer my question:

> **Vero:** *She invents everything!*

> **Meredith:** *She invents everything?*

> **Susana:** *Tell her.*

> **Vero:** *She can invent anything. The other day she made ribs in barbecue. She put a thousand things in it. Whatever she has at hand; she adds and complements flavors. She uses whatever she has, whatever she has bought.*[70]

Almost as a way to prove her ingenuity, her subtle intelligence, García viuda de Melo gets her daughter to testify to her inventive nature. While she did share very specific recipes with me, she recalled them all by memory. The source of García viuda de Melo's inventive *sazón* is her skillful business sense. As she says, she has to cook food that goes a long way since people like to eat a lot for very little money. Susana García viuda de Melo gives us yet another social manifestation of her *sazón*'s sensory-logic.

I close by changing the question I asked at the beginning: "What is the *sazón*?" to "How does one develop a *sazón*?" The *sazón* is the ability to "seize power over one part of oneself" through the epistemology of all our senses, which in turn helps us regain the body as a center of knowledge.[71] The power of the *sazón* to conceptualize and articulate aspects of social reality has been overlooked by privileging the faculties of sight and hearing. These faculties are of fundamental importance in a textually and visually based society like ours. Yet, to categorize the faculties of smell, taste, and touch as less valuable blinds us to the richness and complexity of the ordinary aspects of life, such as food, that make our personal and collective lives meaningful. The epistemologies of all the senses are not only important when studying non-Western societies, they are crucial when studying all societies. Taste and sound and smell, Stoller points out, "are all part of one's experience, [of] one's knowledge of the world, knowledge every bit as important—sometimes more so—than the facts one articulates mentally or verbally."[72] In numerous theoretical and philosophical arguments contesting the privilege sight has had in Western thought, theorists and philosophers formulate their analysis in a model of binary oppositions: the so-called lower senses, taste, smell, and touch, and the "higher" ones, sight and sound.[73] The first set expresses living experiences while the latter is viewed as the senses that assist in obtaining scientific proof; thus, sight is needed for discursive textual expression. The grassroots theorists from the *charlas* participate actively in the culture of the *sazón*, which rejects the binarism of higher and lower senses.

NOTES

1. ***Irma:*** *El arroz se dora, que vaya apenas medio ponièndose cafecito. Entonces cuando yá está [a] ese tiempo el arroz, entonces nada más le vacias la salsa [de jitomate] y le pones el agua. Y pues tienes que saber cuanta agua le tienes que poner. Porque si le pones mucha te va a quedar aguado y si le pones poquita va a quedar crudo.*

   Maria Luisa: *Y, ¿cómo sabes qué tanta agua?*

   Irma: *Pues yo pienso que eso se aprende. Porque yo nunca la mido. Yo la pongo y me queda a la perfección. Yo creo que aprendí bien. Yo la siento. Yo le hago así [le muevo] a la [olla].*

   Meredith: *En la vista, yo creo, ¿no?*

   Irma: *Nó, pienso que en la mano. Porque yo le muevo al arroz y yo sé cuando le falta agua o cuando yá está bien. Al ponerle el agua yo le muevo. Yo sé. No sé como sé. Eso si no te puedo explicar.*

2. Y ya mi prima me enseñó que hacer jamón con piña. Ensalada de macaróne. Costillas en barbecue. Cositas que yo no hubiera aprendido porque uno no las come allá [en el pueblo].

3. Pues [es saber] hacer algo mi'ja, ¿no? Digo yo, a pesar que yo no era de alli del pueblo, de que yo era según de donde no se hacen esas cosas, ¿no? Tú sabes se va y se compran las tortillas. Y pues se sorprendieron [las hermanas de tu papá] porque no creían que yo fuera a saber echar tortillas.

4. Al poner la sal, la agarro con mis dedos y allí le calculo perfectamente bien la sal, en el nombre de Dios. Siempre digo, en le nombre de Dios. Sin querer por inercia lo hago, ¿no? Digo, es una costumbre mía, no. Yo siempre evoco a Dios. O me está bendiciendo los alimentos o el tantéo. Soy tan bruta que digo, "a ver en el nombre de Dios." Es algo que yo hago, nadie me lo enseñó. A lo mejor como yo estaba tan chiquilla cuando empecé a guisar con mi tia. Cuando me dejó mi mamá allí [con la tía] tenía yo como siete años. Así que me tenia que subir a un banco, una sillita de esas de madera chiquitas, para alcanzar la estufa y la olla. Porque la estufa y la olla, ya no alcanzaba yo la cazerola. Y en el metate, molía yo el jitomate, o lo que fuera para la sopa o para el guisado, ¿no? Y yo creo que quizás eso fue el orígen de la cruz. Porque a lo mejor era tanto mi miedo a que no me quedaran bien las cosas, y me fueran a zumbar. Entonces inconcientemente yo decía, "ay Diosito Santo, qué me quede bien." Con el

miedo aquel. Sólo Dios me podia ayudar pare que no le fallara yo a lo que tenía que hacer, verdad. A la receta que me había dado mi tia.

5. A mí me han dicho "tú tienes buen sazón. ¿Por qué no pones un negocio de comida?" Nó. Yo nó. Yo guisar para un restaruante, pars gente que no conozco, no me llama la atención.

6. Yo pongo a cocer mis frijoles nada más le pongo un chorrito de aceite, y un pedazo de cebolla, y la suficente agua. Para no echarle agua. ¡Para nada! Porque el chiste es que el agua [que le pones al prinicpio] te alcance para cocerlos. Entonces le pongo la suficente agua, y los tapo y ya a que se cuezan. Cuando yá están cocidos, los checo de vez en cuando. Cuando yá están cocidos, los checo de vez en cuando. Cuando yá están cocidos así reventaditos, reventaditos, reventaditos, agarro mi salecita y en forma de cruz se la pongo. Le pruebo. Le faltó, otra cruzecita. Y yá los pruebo, y ya están bien, los dejo hervir otro ratito y les apago. Tú te comes un plato así de la olla y te salen riquísimos. Y si tú los coces en la otra olla exprés no tienen el mismo sabor.

7. De la Cruz, *The Answer/La Respuesta*, 74. "Pues ¿que os pudiera contar, Señora, de los secretos naturales que he descubierto estando guisando? Veo que un huevo se une y fríe en la manteca o aceite y, por contrario, se despedaza en el almíbar; ver que para que el azúcar se conserve fluida basta echarle una muy mínima parte de agua en que haya estado membrillo u otra fruta agria; ver que la yema y clara de un mismo huevo son tan contrarias, que en los unos, que sirven para el azúcar, sirve cada una de por sí y juntos nó. Por no cansaros con tales frialdades, que sólo refiero por daros entera noticia de mi natural y creo que os causará risa; pero, señora, ¿qué podemos saber las mujeres sino filosofías de cocina? Bien dijo Lupercio Leonardo, que bien se puede filosofar y aderezar la cena. Y yo suelo decir viendo estas cosillas: Si Aristóteles hubiera guisado, mucho más hubiera escrito."

8. De la Cruz, *The Answer/La Respuesta*, 35–36.

9. Heldke, "Foodmaking as a Thoughtful Practice," 206.

10. Pratt, *Native Pragmatism*, 18.

11. Stoller, *Taste of Ethnographic Things*, 8.

12. Korsemeyer, *Making Sense of Taste*, 11.

13. Ibid., 19.

14. Ibid., 28.

15. Stoller, *Taste of Ethnographic Things*, 8.

16. Quoted in Lefebvre, *Production of Space*, 139.

17. Ibid.

18. Korsemeyer, *Making Sense of Taste*, 85.

19. Quoted in Stoller, *Taste of Ethnographic Things*, 8.

20. Classen, Howes, and Synnott, *Aroma*, 5.

21. Ibid.

22. See Stoller, *Embodying Colonial Memories* (1995) and *Tastes of Ethnographic Things* (1989).

23. Classen, Howes, and Synnott, *Aroma*, 4.

24. Korsemeyer, *Making Sense of Taste*, 31.

25. Ibid.

26. Grosz, *Space, Time, and Perversion*, 26.

27. The *sazón* adds to the ways cross-cultural perspectives illustrate how all theories come out of their specific location and that some are not necessarily universal while others are specific to a particular group. Carole M. Counihan's *The Anthropology of Food and Body: Gender, Meaning, and Power* (1999) and James J. Winchester's *Aesthetics across the Color Line* (2002) talk about this particular benefit of cross-cultural research.

28. Stoller, *Taste of Ethnographic Things*, 9.

29. In *Distinction: A Social Critique of the Judgement of Taste* (1984) Bourdieu illustrates this point by indicating how the faculty of taste to judge aesthetic value is connected to economic factors and education.

30. Since Greek times, two manifestations in efforts to control the body, the vessel of moral decline, have been fasting or chastity. Carole M. Counihan, in *Anthropology of Food and Body*, speaks of such control, as it has related to women, as the "Western Women's Prodigious Fasting." In an effort to save their souls, medieval women engaged in a "holiness" fasting; Victorian women fasted for "daintiness"; the modern women fast for "thinness," 111.

31. Curtin and Heldke, *Cooking, Eating, Thinking*, xiii.

32. De Certeau, *Practice of Everyday Life*.

33. Narayan, "Eating Cultures," 64.

34. Lupton, *Food, the Body, and the Self*, 13.

35. Es que es según la costumbre. Aquí los americanos son gente más civilizada, es lo correcto, ¿no? La medida. Pero cuando uno no tiene tiempo de medir, o cuando uno no tiene esa curiosidad de medir, no importa. Porque tú la tanteada la tienes en la mano y en el ojo. Donde pones el ojo o pones el tantéo, ya estuvo. Pero si tú no tienes el tantéo, pues necesitas medir. Pero si tienes el tanteo, no necesitas medir.

36. Massey, *Space, Place, and Gender*, 6.

37. Para dejar que el elote se haga maíz lo tienes que dejar en la milpa, en la planta, hasta que se ponga amarillo, hasta que se seca la hoja y luego se cortan las mazorcas. Y luego se desgrana, se coce y luego se hace el nixtamal. Se cose con agua y cal. Y tienes que saber cuanta cantidad de cal, que tan fuerte tiene que estar porque sí te pasas de cal te queda amarillo y entonces sabe feo. Este, tienes que saber que tanta cal se le pone al agua y tienes que saber el punto de la cocida también. Para saber si ya están los granitos del maíz cocidos, agarras un granito y si ya se le quita el pellejito, ya está cocido. Y ya lo quitas de la lumbre. Allí se queda para otro dia. Otro día lo sacas, lo enjuagas y lo mueles.

38. **Meredith:** *Y de cantidades, ¿cómo sabes? Dices, "le echo estó y le echo el otro." ¿Pero cuánto? ¿Cómo sabes qué tanta cantidad?*

    Alma: *No sé decir yo de cantidades porque es algo que yo le calculo.*

    Meredith: *¿Cómo le calculas? ¿Cómo sabes más o menos?*

    Alma: *Pos' la porción que voy a hacer. Cebolla. Le pongo una cebolla si voy a hacer la olla grande. Le pongo sal, y eso es al gusto. Cualquiera le puede calcular al gusto la sal. A muchos les gusta salado, a muchos les gusta no salado. Chile. Usualmente la bolsa de chile. Si lo quieres muy picoso, dos bolsas.*

39. **Meredith:** *Y, ¿por qué se amargan? ¿Le pasa lo que al ajo?*

    Esperanza: *Andale, le pasa lo que al ajo. A la hora de pasarse [de dorado], se amarga, se quema. Y entonces ya el pipián tiene otro color y otro sabor. No le pones la gran cosa. [Pero] es tan sabroso que yo a donde voy de visita que me toca llevar un platillo, "Ay señora, a usted el toca le pipián verde." "Esperanza a tí te toca el pipián verde." ¿Por que? Porque a todo el mundo le gusta el pipián verde.*

    Meredith: *¿Tú lo has comido de otras personas?*

    Esperanza: *Sí.*

Meredith: Y. ¿Cómo les queda?

Esperanza: Pues no es igual.

40. Farb and Armelagos, *Consuming Passions*, 12.
41. Bauer, "Millers and Grinders," 6.
42. Gabaccia, *We Are What We Eat*, 222. Other food literature that deals with the practices of eating the "Other" range from discussion of culinary tourism (see the works of Lucy Long) to culinary colonialism. Also see Helkde (2003) and Narayan (1997).

43. *Alma:* Nunca le he medido el agua. Pero la receta para que no te queden prietos es que al hervir le tienes que bajar [al fuego] y taparlos. Y solitos se cocen y no [hay que] agregarles más agua. O sea se tarda más en cocerse pero quedan güeritos. O sea cuando tengo ganas de frijoles americanos los hago asi. Cuando tengo ganas de frijoles mexicanos los hago a la carrera. Les estoy eche y eche agua para que se cocan rapido y salen prietos.

Meredith: ¿Pero por qué unos son a la americana y otros a la mexicana?

Alma: Los americanos son güeritos y los mexicanos son prietitos. . . . O sea depende del tiempo que tengas.

44. *Meredith:* Oiga, ¿cómo le iba cuándo vendía hot dogs?

Yaya: A veces bien, a veces mal. Buena al hot dog se le gana nomás necesita uno un buen lugar. Tu encuentras un buen lugar donde haya gente hispana, pero por lo regular mexicana porque si es salvadoreña no vendes nada.

Meredith: ¿Por qué cree usted que ese es el caso?

Yaya: Porque los salvadoreños, ellos sólo compran lo tradicional de su tierra. Las pupusas, los platános fritos con frijoles. Todo eso. Pero el hotdog no se vende. Pero donde hay raza mexicana, eso es bien vendible.

Meredith: ¿Por qué si los hot dogs no se producto de nosotros?

Yaya: No, pero son perros calientes de nuestro país. Nomás volteas el nombre y son perros calientes de nuestro país. . . . Antes vendía hot dogs. Ahora ya tengo mucho tiempo que no vendo. Con eso que me cambie de donde vivía. Ahorita hay puro salvadoreño donde vivo.

45. Grosz, *Space, Time, and Perversion*, 30.
46. Bordo, *Unbearable Weight*, 38.
47. Lupton, *Food, the Body, and the Self*, 13.
48. Stoller, *Taste of Ethnographic Things*, 29.
49. De Certeau, Giard, and Mayol, *Practice of Everyday Life:* Volume Two: *Living and Cooking* 156.

50. *Alma:* Hacen muchas enchiladas [y] las meten al horno y luego ponen todo y todos se sirven. A mí no me gusta.

Duvi: Pues nomás porque es más trabajo estar haciéndolas. Pero el saborcito, el saborcito calientito.

Meredith: Pero de la otra manera se sientan todos a comer al mismo tiempo.

Alma: Si, [pero] a mí no me gustan así. A mí me gusto que estén casi bien doraditas.

Meredith: ¿Y a qué horas comes tú?

Duvi: Al final.

Alma: Al final. Cuando terminan todos, preparo las mías. O trato [de hacerlas] rápido para que quede una de las personas a comer conmigo—

Duvi: Y en el micro, mi'ja. A lo mejor en el micro, sí.

Alma: No, donde funcionaría muy bien es en los hornitos chiquitos. Quizás en el hornito sí, porque quedarían igual. Los tamales los he calentado en el hornito y quedan muy ricos. Mejor que en el microwave.

51. O sea, es algo que disfruta hacer [mi mamá], cocinar. Algo que a mi no. O sea cuando yo estaba en la casa que me decía, "tienes que venir a ver para cuando te cases." Yo odiaba estar en la cocina. Nunca, nunca me ha gustado.

52. De Certeau, Giard, and Mayol, *Practice of Everyday Life:* Volume Two: *Living and Cooking,* 151.

53. Ibid., 157.

54. Ibid., 202.

55. Ibid., 201.

56. El metate que mi tía tiene es un metate que usó su abuelita. Mi bisabuclita. Tiene como ciento treinta años—¡más! Si mi tía tiene noventa y se lo regalaron a su abuelita. ¡Imagínate!

57. The specific image of transmitting a part of one's self through the use of a *metate* is by no means only operative in the hands of the women I am mentioning. We only need to recall Laura Esquivel's *Como agua para chocolate* (*Like Water for Chocolate*). Audre Lorde in *Zami* uses the mortar and pestle as a way of feeling the presence of her own body and as a way of transmitting an essential part of the person into the food being prepared.

58. Mi mamá . . . sabe hacer un mole tan rico. Y todo lo muele en el metate. Yo le traté de ayudar en el noventa, cuando fuimos todos. Hizo mole pa' todos, pues. Le traté de ayudar a moler. Yo nomás veía que le molía tan fácil en el metate. Y le dije, "a ver amacita, deje ayudarle." Y me salía todo el chile pa' fuera. . . . Le empujaba, le tallaba pero salían los pedazos de chile. ¡Chilote! Y ella le molía [e] iba saliendo así remolidito, remolidito.

59. Carne con chile. Este, doraba la carne, y luego ella siempre molía los chiles guajillos y le ponía un chile pasilla . . . ella los molía en el metate. Yo pienso que eso es lo que le daba el sabor, que ella lo hacía siempre en el metate. Aunque hubiera licuadora, . . . ella de todas maneras molía sus chiles, y, este, el nixtamal en el metate. Yo pienso que eso era lo que le daba el sabor porque de otra manera es la misma cosa que nosotras hacemos. Lavas la carne, este, pones los chiles a cocer. Pero la única diferencia es que los pones en la licuadora. Y ella no. Ella siempre los hacía en el metate.

60. Lefebvre, *Production of Space,* 215.

61. Mauss, *The Gift,* 10.

62. Cuando vamos, . . . le encanta hacernos mole. Y usa el metate. Ahorita ella tiene su licuadora, porque también ya está grande. Pero a ella le gusta molerlo en el metate.

63. De Certeau, Giard, and Mayol, *Practice of Everyday Life:* Volume Two: *Living and Cooking*, 212.

64. Yo nunca apunto medidas. Tú también haces las cosas al tanteo. ¿O tú sí usas medidas? No creo que vayas a la receta. [Yo] no me baso al libro y estar viendo lo que va [en la receta].

65. *Alma: Los ingredientes. Pos' se prepara la harina, el huevo, el este para la elevadura. Y, este, se raspa la zanahoría y naranja, la cascarita de la naranja raspada. Y se mete al horno. Y quedaba bien rico.*

Meredith: Y ¿dónde aprendiste a hacer éste pastel?

Alma: Por una receta de un libro. Pero pregúntame que lo vuelva a hacer ya no me acuerdo muy bien. Pero allá lo hacía mucho.

66. See Elizabeth Grosz's distinction between corporal knowledge and inscribed knowledge in *Space, Time, and Perversion* (1995).

67. *Meredith: Oye, ¿y todas estas recetas, las [tienes] en un libro o [te] las [sabes] de memoria?*

Esperanza: Nó, de memoria. Yo no las tengo en recetas. Yo me las sé de memoria.

68. Yo vine a ver libros de cocina hasta acá contigo, yo creo. Y aquí en las casas donde ando trabajando. Y allá en el restaruante donde entré [a trabajar] el Bay Window.

69. *Meredith: ¿Platíqueme un poquito, bueno, no sé si le gusta platicar de sus recetas?*

Susana: De mis recetas, sí como no.

Meredith: ¿Tiene alguna receta que uste ha inventado? Que diga, "esto es mio."

70. *Vero: ¡Inventa todo!*

Meredith: ¿Inventa todo?

Susana: Dile.

Vero: Te puede inventar todo. El otro día se puso hacer que costillitas al barbecue. Y le pone veinte mil cocas . . . lo que tenga a la mano le pone y le complementa. Ahora sí, de lo que tenga y haya comprado.

71. De Certeau, Giard, and Mayol, *Practice of Everyday Life:* Volume Two: *Living and Cooking*, 213.

72. Stoller, *Embodying Colonial Memories*, 25.

73. See for example Stoler's *Embodying Colonial Memories*. Lefebvre's *Production of Space*, and De Certeau, Giard, and Mayol's, *Practice of Everyday Life:* Volume Two: *Living and Cooking*.

REFERNCES CITED

Bauer AJ. 1990. Millers and grinders: Technology and household economy in Meso-America. *Agricultural History* 64(1):1–17.

Bordo S. 2003. *Unbearable Weight: Feminism, Western Culture, and the Body*. 10th anniversary edition. Berkeley: University of California Press.

Bourdieu P. 1984. *Distinction: A Social Critique of the Judgement of Taste*. Cambridge, MA: Harvard University Press.

Classen C, Howes D, Synnott A. 1994. *Aroma: The Cultural History of Smell*. New York: Routledge.

Counihan CM. 1999. *The Anthropology of Food and Body*. New York: Routledge.

Curtin DW, Heldke LM. Ed. 1992. *Cooking, Eating, Thinking: Transformative Philosophies of Food*. Bloomington: Indiana University Press.

de Certeau M. 1984. *The Practice of Everyday Life*. Rendall S. Trans. Berkeley: University of California Press.

de Certeau M, Giard L, Mayol P. 1998. *The Practice of Everyday Life*: Volume Two: *Living and Cooking*. Tomasik TJ. Trans. Minneapolis: University of Minnesota Press.

de la Cruz SJI. 1994. *The Answer/La Respuesta*. Arenal E, Powell A. Ed. and trans. New York: The Feminist Press.

Esquivel L. 1993. *Como agua para chocolate*. New York: Doubleday.

Farb P, Armelagos G. 1982. *Consuming Passions: The Anthropology of Eating*. Boston: Houghton Mifflin.

Gabaccia DR. 1998. *We Are What We Eat: Ethnic Food and the Making of Americans*. Cambridge, MA: Harvard University Press.

Grosz E. 1995. *Space, Time, and Perversion*. New York: Routledge.

Heldke LM. 1992. Foodmaking as a thoughtful practice. In: *Cooking, Eating, Thinking: Transformative Philosophies of Food*. Curtin DW, Heldke LM. Ed. Bloomington: Indiana University Press. Pp. 203–229.

Heldke LM. 2003. *Exotic Appetites: Ruminations of a Food Adventurer*. New York: Routledge.

Korsmeyer C. 1999. *Making Sense of Taste: Food and Philosophy*. Ithaca, NY: Cornell University Press.

Lefebvre H. 1991. *The Production of Space*. Nicholson-Smith D. Trans. Cambridge, MA: Blackwell Publishers.

Lorde A. 1982. *Zami: A New Spelling of My Name*. New York: Crossing Press.

Lupton D. 1996. *Food, the Body, and the Self*. London: Sage Publications.

Massey D. 1994. *Space, Place, and Gender*. Minneapolis: University of Minnesota Press.

Mauss M. [1925] 1967. *The Gift*. New York: Norton.

Narayan U. 1995. Eating cultures: Incorporation, identity, and Indian food. *Social Identities* 1(64).

Narayan U. 1997. *Dislocating Cultures: Identities, Traditions, and Third-World Feminism*. New York: Routledge.

Pratt SL. 2002. *Native Pragmatism: Rethinking the Roots of American Philosophy*. Bloomington: Indiana University Press.

Stoller P. 1989. *The Taste of Ethnographic Things: The Senses in Anthropology*. Philadelphia: University of Pennsylvania Press.

Stoller P. 1995. *Embodying Colonial Memories*. New York: Routledge.

Preventing Obesity in Mexican-American Children and Adolescents

Frederick Trowbridge and Fernando Mendoza

INTRODUCTION

Childhood obesity has become a worldwide concern because of its epidemic proportions and its growing link to type 2 diabetes and other chronic health conditions. Over the past two decades, there has been an increase in childhood and adolescent obesity to an unprecedented level. During the 1960s–1970s, the prevalence of obesity in children and adolescents in the United States was relatively stable at about 4–7 percent. However, during the 1980s the obesity prevalence doubled, with 11 percent of children and adolescents having body mass index (BMI) levels over the 95th percentile by the early 1990s (CDC, 2005b). In the latest National Health and Nutrition Examination Survey (NHANES) 2003–2004 (Ogden et al., 2006), childhood and adolescent obesity prevalence increased to 17 percent, which is triple the rate in NHANES I (1971–1974) and NHANES II (1976–1980) (Hedley et al., 2004). This dramatic increase in prevalence has driven childhood and adolescent obesity to a prominent position in the clinical and research arenas of child health. Moreover, as the links between obesity and its co-morbidities (e.g., type 2 diabetes, asthma, hypertension, sleep apnea, skeletal-muscular disorders, self-esteem and mental health disorders, and other chronic illnesses) have become more evident, the awareness of the long-term health effects of child and adolescent obesity has raised concerns at all levels of child health policy.

Addressing the problem of obesity in Mexican-American children and adolescents will require consideration of the unique historical and demographic characteristics of Mexican Americans. Since the 1500s Mexican Americans have lived in what is now the southwestern United States and have maintained a continuing interchange of culture with Mexico. Today, Mexicans continue to immigrate to locations across the United States, and to maintain their

Frederick Trowbridge and Fernando Mendoza, "Preventing Obesity in Mexican-American Children and Adolescents," first published in *Joint U.S.-Mexico Workshop on Preventing Obesity in Children and Youth of Mexican Origin*, ed. María Oria and Kristin Sawyer. Washington, D.C.: National Academies Press, 2007. Reprinted with permission from the National Academy of Sciences, Courtesy of the National Academies Press, Washington, D.C.

cultural ties. Currently, one in five children in the United States lives in an immigrant family; they are either first- or second-generation children of immigrant parents (NRC/IOM,1998). The country of origin for the largest proportion of these children is Mexico. In 2000, 39 percent of children in families new to the United States were Mexican—no other country contributes more than 4 percent (Hernandez, 2004).

The substantial and ongoing interchange of people and culture between the United States and Mexico makes it clear that addressing childhood obesity in the Mexican-American community requires an approach that recognizes the common social, cultural, economic, and possibly genetic factors that contribute to childhood obesity in both Mexican-American and Mexican children and adolescents. At the same time, the influence of the substantially different social, cultural, and economic environment in which Mexican-Americans living in the United States find themselves must also be taken into account. This paper reviews the prevalence and trends in obesity in Mexican-American children and youth and considers the multiple factors that may contribute to this growing health problem. The paper then provides an overview of current intervention strategies and programs and proposes actions that may offer the greatest potential for success in preventing and controlling the obesity epidemic.

EXTENT AND CONSEQUENCES OF OBESITY IN MEXICAN-AMERICAN CHILDREN AND YOUTH

Data from national surveys clearly demonstrate a high and increasing prevalence of childhood obesity in the United States (Ogden et al., 2002, 2006; Hedley et al., 2004). Obesity is particularly prevalent among Mexican-American children and youth. Moreover, Mexican-American children have a high prevalence of abdominal obesity, which may put them at elevated risk for type 2 diabetes and cardiovascular disease (CVD). High rates of obesity also may indicate that Mexican-American children and adolescents are more exposed to the negative impacts of obesity on their social and emotional health. Finally, since many Mexican-American children and youth depend on publicly funded health care programs such as Medicaid, the high prevalence of obesity will place increasing demands on health care providers serving Hispanic populations and thus will have significant implications for the funding needs of these programs.

MEASUREMENT OF OBESITY IN CHILDREN AND YOUTH

BODY MASS INDEX (BMI)

BMI is recommended widely as an appropriate measure of obesity in children older than 2 years of age (Daniels et al., 1997; Pietrobelli et al., 1998). This indicator is calculated easily from simple measurements of height and weight and is associated closely with indicators of cardiovascular disease (CVD) risk (Katzmarzyk et al., 2004). In addition, analysis of BMI data is facilitated by the availability of gender-specific reference data developed by the CDC for determining BMI-for-age percentiles (Kuczmarski et al., 2002). Reference curves based on an international data set derived from large, nationally representative surveys of child growth from six countries also are available (Cole et al., 2000). These reference curves are designed to merge smoothly with the BMI values for adults defining *overweight* as having a BMI between 25 to 29.9 kg/m^2 and *obese* as having a BMI equal to or greater than 30 kg/m^2. For consistency between the IOM report and this paper, obesity in children and youth is defined as having a BMI equal to or greater than age- and gender-specific 95th percentile of the BMI charts developed by the Centers for Disease Control and Prevention (CDC) in 2000. Being at-risk for obesity is defined as having a BMI between the age- and gender-specific 85th and 95th percentiles of the CDC BMI charts (IOM, 2005).

However, BMI also has recognized limitations as an obesity indicator. The relationship of BMI to body fat in children varies in relation to age, maturational stage, gender, race, and fat distribution, so that a given BMI will not reflect an equivalent level of body fat for all individuals (Daniels et al., 1997). Despite these limitations, BMI remains a useful and practical indicator for clinical assessment and for characterizing obesity prevalence in population-based studies.

WAIST CIRCUMFERENCE

Waist circumference is a more specific indicator of abdominal fat, and it appears to perform at least as well as BMI in identifying children with a clustering of CVD risk factors (Katzmarzyk et al., 2004). Among the 4–17-year-old children and youth who were sampled in the NHANES III (1988–1994), waist-to-height ratio actually performed better than BMI in identifying those with elevated CVD risk factors (Kahn et al., 2005). A 10-year cohort study beginning when children were 9 and 10 years old found that waist circumference and triglyceride level were significant predictors of the metabolic syndrome[1] at ages 18 to 19 years. In this study, BMI was not a significant predictor once waist circumference was included in the multivariate model (Morrison et al., 2005). The importance of abdominal obesity as a risk factor for CVD in adults was highlighted in a recent study that found that having an elevated waist-to-hip ratio was associated more strongly with myocardial infarction than having an elevated BMI (Yusuf et al., 2005). The population-attributable risk of myocardial infarction for the top two quintiles of waist-to-hip ratio was 24.3 percent versus only 7.7 percent for the top two quintiles of BMI.

Descriptive data showing percentile distributions of waist circumference have been developed for 2–8-year-old African-American, European-American, and Mexican-American children based on data from NHANES III (Fernandez et al., 2004). In the same NHANES III data set, the waist circumference-to-height ratio did not vary significantly in relation to sex or age group, making it feasible to use a single set of cutoffs for classifying children of both sexes and all ages from 4 to 17 years (Kahn et al., 2005). The strong association of increased waist circumference with CVD risk factors and the availability of reference data support the use of waist circumference indicators, in addition to BMI, as valid and practical tools for assessing obesity and associated CVD risk in children and adolescents. However, additional research is needed to confirm the risks associated with abdominal obesity in different age, gender, and ethnic groups (especially Mexican and Mexican-American children and youth) and the usefulness of waist circumference as an indicator, alone or in combination with BMI, in identifying abdominal obesity in these different groups of children and adolescents.

OBESITY PREVALENCE AND TRENDS

PREVALENCE

Since the late 1970s, there has been a dramatic increase in the prevalence of obesity among children and youth across all racial and ethnic groups in the United States. Data from national surveys indicate that the prevalence of obesity has more than doubled for children ages 2–5 years and adolescents ages 12–19 years, and obesity rates have more than tripled for children ages 6–11 years (Ogden et al., 2002). Prevalence estimates based on the National Longitudinal Survey of Youth data from 1986–1998 in children ages 4–12 years provide a similar picture of the increasing prevalence of obesity (Strauss and Pollack, 2001).

An elevated prevalence of obesity is particularly evident for Mexican-American boys. In NHANES 2003–2004 (Ogden et al., 2006), Mexican-American boys ages 2–5 and 6–11 years had a higher prevalence of obesity than boys of any other race or ethnic group, while obesity prevalence for male adolescents was similar to other ethnic groups. In the 2003–2004 NHANES, Mexican-American girls ages 2–5 and 6–11 years had a prevalence of obesity that was less than that of African-American girls but greater than that of non-Hispanic White girls, while obesity prevalence for female Mexican-American adolescents was similar to non-Hispanic Whites. Additional research is needed to assess the underlying attitudes and diet and physical activity practices that may trigger these age, gender, and ethnic group differences.

It is of interest to compare the prevalence of obesity in Mexican-American children and adolescents with their counterparts in Mexico. Data from the Mexican National Nutrition Survey (1999) (Rivera et al., 2001) and the Mexican National Health Survey (2000) (Olaiz et al., 2003) were analyzed using the same CDC reference criteria to define obesity (López Ridaura et al., 2006; del Rio-Navarro et al., 2004; Kuczmarski et al., 2002). Overall, results indicated that, except for the preschool age group, Mexican children had a lower prevalence of obesity than ethnically similar children in the United States surveyed in 1999–2000 (Ogden et al., 2006). Obesity prevalence in 2–5-year-old Mexican children was similar to their Mexican-American counterparts. However, older Mexican children and adolescents had an obesity prevalence that was only half or one-third of the prevalence seen in Mexican-American children and adolescents.

These results in children and adolescents from ethnically similar backgrounds suggest that environmental factors in the United States exert a significant influence on the growth and weight status of Mexican-American children and youth.

ABDOMINAL OBESITY PREVALENCE

Abdominal obesity appears to be a particular concern for Mexican adults, children, and youth. Data from the Mexican National Health Survey conducted in 2000 indicate a high prevalence of abdominal obesity in Mexican adults based on waist circumference measurements, with a reported prevalence of 46.3 percent in men (waist circumference ≥ 94 cm and 81.4 percent in women (waist circumference ≥ 80 cm) (Sanchez-Castill et al., 2005). Abdominal obesity was elevated even in women of normal weight, with co-morbidities relating better to waist circumference than to BMI. Moreover, the high prevalence of abdominal obesity in Mexican men and women was associated with a prevalence of diabetes and hypertensic similar to or exceeding levels observed in the non-Hispanic White population in NHANES III (1988–1994).

These observations of increased abdominal obesity in Mexican adults parallel the finding of increased abdominal girth in Mexican-American children and youth. In the NHANES III survey, 13.9 percent of Mexican-American children were classified as having a waist circumference-to-height ratio category that exceeded their BMI category, whereas only 7 percent of non-Hispanic Blacks and 9.48 percent of the overall sample were so classified

TABLE C-1 Prevalence of Obesity in Non-Hispanic White, Mexican-American, and Mexican Children: 1999–2000

Age/Gender Group	NHANES 1999–2000 Non-Hispanic White	NHANES 1999–2000[a] Mexican-American	Mexican National Nutrition Survey[b] 1999	Mexican National Health Survey[c] 2000
Boys				
2–5	6.9	13.1	11.1	
6–11	11.9	26.7	9.1	
12–17	11.8	27.2		10.6
Girls				
2–5	10.5	8.7	9.7	
6–11	11.6	19.8	8.5	
12–17	11.0	19.3		9.3

NOTE: Obesity is defined as greater than 95th percentile of BMI (Kuczmarski et al., 2002).
[a]Ogden et al. (2002).
[b]Rivera et al. (2002).
[c]del Rio-Navarro et al. (2004). Data represent average prevalence values for children 12 to 17 years.

(Kahn et al., 2005). A separate analysis of NHANES III data found that the smoothed 90th percentile of waist circumference for Mexican-American boys was consistently higher than that observed for either African-American boys or European-American boys. The 90th percentile for Mexican-American girls also was consistently higher than that of European-American girls at all ages and greater than that of African-American girls up to 9 years of age. Analysis of waist circumference data from the 1999–2000 NHANES survey also found a consistent pattern of higher mean waist circumference values for Mexican-American children (Ford et al., 2004).

These findings of increased waist circumference suggest that Mexican-American children and youth, and particularly Mexican-American boys at all ages, may be at an increased risk of co-morbidities associated with abdominal obesity, including type 2 diabetes.

HISTORICAL AND CURRENT OBESITY TRENDS

Obesity among Mexican-American children is not a new finding. A review of growth studies on Mexican-American children and youth during 1920–1980 (based primarily on immigrant and low-income Mexican Americans) showed a high prevalence of short stature and low weight that was indicative of undernutrition (Malina et al., 1986). However, by the 1970s and early 1980s, regional studies in this review indicated a higher-than-expected level of obesity among Mexican-American children and youth. This increased level of obesity was associated with a shorter stature as compared with non-Hispanic Whites, resulting in a short, plump physique.

Data from NHANES I (1971–1974) demonstrated that differences in BMI between Mexican-American and non-Hispanic children and youth were related significantly to socioeconomic status (SES) (Mendoza and Castillo, 1986). Mexican-American children who had a lower SES had BMIs higher than their non-Hispanic counterparts, but this finding disappeared as SES increased. A combined analysis of NHANES I (1971–1974) and NHANES II (1976–1978) also found that stature was associated directly with SES and that poor children and youth were shorter (Martorell et al., 1988b). Overall, Mexican-American children and youth in this study were shown to have a short, plump physique, and the data suggested they also had increased upper body fat (Martorell et al., 1988a). Height comparisons between Mexican-American children and non-Hispanic White children showed differences related to SES, although a similar association was not seen for Mexican-American adolescents. These observations suggest that short stature in lower SES Mexican-American children was likely to be related to less adequate nutrition early in life or even during the prenatal period. Since an SES effect was not seen in adolescents it may be that other factors, possibly genetic, are more influential after puberty.

Data analysis from the Hispanic Health and Nutrition Examination Survey (HHANES) (1982–1984) indicated that Mexican-American children showed a higher-than-expected proportion of children above the 90th percentile for BMI between ages 6–11 years—with several year-groups showing twice the expected level—although adolescents showed more variability in the prevalence of obesity (Martorell et al., 1989). Further analyses of the HHANES showed that obesity was associated with increased centralized upper body adiposity and was not a result of having a different body proportion as compared with non-Hispanic Whites (Kaplowitz et al., 1989; Martorell et al., 1988a). In summary, data from HHANES confirmed findings from early studies, indicating that Mexican-American children had increased levels of obesity.

The upward trend in obesity prevalence in Mexican-American children has continued in recent years. Between NHANES III (1988–1994) and NHANES (2003–2004), the prevalence of obesity in adolescent Mexican-American boys ages 12–19 years increased by 4.2 percent. Among girls, the largest increases were noted in non-Hispanic White and African-American adolescents, although obesity also increased in Mexican-American girls (NCHS, 2004; Ogden et al., 2006). It is interesting to note that reported obesity prevalence in male Mexican-American adolescents 12–19 years old decreased from 27.2 percent in 1999–2000 to 18.3 percent in 2003–2004, and in female adolescents from 19.3 percent in 1999–2000 to 14.1 percent in 2003–2004 (Ogden et al., 2006). The authors note that subgroup estimates by sex, age, and race/ethnicity are less precise than overall estimates due to smaller sample sizes, so that these prevalence estimates must be interpreted with caution.

It is interesting to note that as obesity prevalence has increased over the last several decades, the linear growth of Mexican-American children and adolescents has shown relatively little change. Linear growth improved from the 1960s to 1980s when HHANES was conducted, suggesting that Mexican-American children and youth had not previously been achieving their full height potential (Martorell et al., 1989). Analysis of more recent data indicates that although weight-for-age and BMI percentiles of Mexican-American children increased between HHANES (1982-1984) and NHANES III (1988–1994), stature-for-age percentiles were largely unchanged (Ryan et al., 1999). Moreover, median height-for-age values for Mexican-American children in NHANES III closely paralleled the median of the CDC reference population and thus indicated that Mexican-American children were achieving linear growth similar to the general U.S. population up to early adolescence.

At approximately 13 to 14 years of age, however, the median stature of Mexican-American girls and boys falls to about the 25th percentile of the CDC reference. The reasons for the falloff in linear growth in adolescents are not well defined but might be related to genetic influences such as an earlier onset of puberty. In any case, the pattern of increased weight-for-age in the interval from HHANES to NHANES III, coupled with little change in stature-for-age, has resulted in a higher ratio of weight to height and is reflected in the increased prevalence of elevated BMI values in Mexican-American children and youth. Further research is needed to better understand the underlying causes of this pattern of linear and weight growth as well as the relationship it may have to the development of obesity. It also would be of interest to compare the pattern of weight and stature growth in Mexican-American children and adolescents with the pattern observed in their counterparts in Mexico.

Data from the National Longitudinal Survey of Youth also demonstrate the upward trend in childhood obesity and indicate a more rapid increase among Hispanic and African-American youth when compared to their European-American counterparts (Strauss and Pollack, 2001). Between 1986 and 1998, the annual rate of increase in obesity prevalence in children ages 4–12 years has been estimated at 4.3 percent and 5.8 percent for Hispanic and African-American youth, respectively, when compared to 3.2 percent for European-American youth. Obesity increased more rapidly among children in southern states (6.2 percent per year) when compared with children in northeastern, central, and western states (3.6 percent, 1.8 percent, and 2.2 percent, respectively) (Strauss and Pollack, 2001). This regional difference in prevalence may be related partly to the high prevalence of Hispanics residing in the southern United States.

Trends in waist circumference in children and adolescents also have been observed. In the interval between NHANES III (1988–1994) and NHANES (1999–2000), waist circumference increased significantly among 12–17-year-old adolescents (Ford et al., 2004). The largest increase in this age group was observed among Mexican-American boys, whose mean waist circumference measurements increased by 5.8 cm (from 78 cm to 83.8 cm)—an increase that was larger than that seen in African-American (5.2 cm) or White non-Hispanic boys (0.5 cm). The mean waist circumference of Mexican-American adolescent girls increased by 5 cm (from 76.3 cm to 81.3 cm)—an increase that was greater than that observed for African-American girls (2.9 cm) or European-American girls (3 cm) of the same age group. These findings indicate a significant increase in abdominal obesity among Mexican-American adolescents.

Overall, these data indicate that childhood obesity, and perhaps abdominal obesity in particular, represents a long-term and increasing problem among Mexican-American children and adolescents.

HEALTH AND ECONOMIC IMPACTS OF OBESITY

IMPACT ON PHYSICAL HEALTH

The relationship between obesity and chronic disease risk in adults has been observed and documented widely. Obesity increases the risk of many conditions including hypertension, CVD, stroke, type 2 diabetes, and certain types of cancer. Since obese children and youth are more likely to be overweight or obese as adults, there is a direct link between childhood obesity and long-term chronic disease risk. Concerns about childhood-onset obesity are supported by documented associations between childhood obesity and increased CVD risk and mortality in adulthood (Srinivasan et al., 2002; Li et al., 2004). Lifetime risk of developing type 2 diabetes for children born in the United States in 2000 has been estimated at 30 percent for boys and 40 percent for girls, with a higher level of risk for ethnic minorities (Narayan, 2003). Although childhood-onset obesity accounts for only 25 percent of adult obesity cases, obesity that is present before a child is 8 years of age and persists into adulthood is associated with severe obesity—defined as a BMI greater than

40 kg/m^2—in adulthood as compared with a BMI of 35 for adult-onset obesity (Freedman et al., 2001). Between 1990 and 2000, severe obesity (which is associated with more serious health complications) more than doubled, increasing from 0.78 percent to 2.2 percent in U.S. adults (Freedman et al., 2002).

Longitudinal data in 5–17-year-old European-American and African-American children indicate that obese children had a significantly increased risk for elevated low-density lipoprotein cholesterol, systolic and diastolic blood pressure, and fasting insulin. Fifty percent of the children with two or more of these risk factors were identified by using obesity (defined as a BMI equal to or greater than the 95th percentile) as a screening tool (Freedman et al., 1999). More recent studies in 126 obese Hispanic children ages 8–13 years found that 90 percent of these children had at least one feature of the metabolic syndrome and 30 percent had three or more risk factors and were diagnosed with the metabolic syndrome (Cruz et al., 2004). Furthermore, a recent analysis of NHANES (1999–2000) found that 12–19-year-old Mexican–American adolescents had a higher prevalence (13 percent) of impaired fasting glucose than either non-Hispanic Black (4.2 percent) or non-Hispanic White adolescents (7 percent) (Williams et al., 2005).

As noted previously, increased waist circumference or waist-to-height ratio has been shown to be as effective as, or even more effective than, BMI in identifying children with multiple CVD risk factors (Katzmarzyk et al., 2004; Kahn et al., 2005). For this reason, the increasing abdominal obesity observed in Mexican-American youth indicates that they may be at particular risk for CVD in adulthood.

The association of obesity with the risk of developing type 2 diabetes in childhood and adolescence is a particularly serious concern. Children and adolescents who develop type 2 diabetes may experience the micro- and macrovascular complications of this disease at younger ages than individuals who develop diabetes in adulthood (Hannon et al., 2005). An increasing incidence of type 2 diabetes was documented in a longitudinal study from 1982–1994 that showed a 10-fold increase—from 0.7 cases per 100,000 per year in 1982 to 7.2 cases per 100,000 per year in 1994—in incidence among 10–19-year-old adolescents (Pinhas-Hamiel et al., 1996).

An analysis of data from NHANES III (1988–1994) and NHANES (1999–2002) showed a higher prevalence of diabetes and impaired glucose tolerance (a pre-diabetic condition) among Mexican-American adults compared with non-Hispanic Whites, which is consistent with data showing that Mexican-American adults are 1.7 times more likely to have diabetes than non-Hispanic White adults (CDC, 2003, 2005a). Similarly, higher rates of type 2 diabetes are being observed in Mexican-American children and adolescents. As an example, a survey of six high schools in Ventura County, California, identified 28 diabetic adolescents—75 percent more than expected (Neufeld et al., 1998). Correlations were found between the Hispanic enrollment in each school and the number of diabetic adolescents as well as between the obesity rates and adolescents with type 2 diabetes and impaired glucose tolerance.

Sleep apnea is another morbidity related to obesity. It has been suggested that Mexican Americans may have a higher prevalence of sleep apnea than other Hispanic subgroups (Strohl and Redline, 1996). Unfortunately, the available data for the prevalence of obstructive sleep apnea among Mexican-American children and adolescents are very limited (R. Pelayo, Stanford University Sleep Center, personal communication, 2005), even though clinical experience in obesity centers suggests that this is a prominent and growing problem (L. Hammer, Stanford University Medical Center, personal communication, 2005).

Asthma is another morbidity associated with childhood obesity. This condition has been reported to occur at a similar rate among Mexican-American children and adolescents surveyed in HHANES and NHANES III when compared with non-Hispanic Whites (NCR/IOM, 1998, 1999). An analysis by generational status of Mexican-American children and adolescents recorded a lower maternal-reported prevalence of asthma among first- and second-generation children when compared with third and later generations (NRC/IOM, 1998). Although these data are self-reported and rely on having access to physicians, the trend of increasing asthma with each generation mirrors the pattern for childhood and adolescent obesity. An evaluation of the prevalence of asthma among Mexican-American children and youth in NHANES III showed an odds ratio of 2.1 (1.4, 2.9) for children with a BMI greater than the 85th percentile (Agredano et al., 2004).

Other physical conditions associated with obesity are abnormal serum lipids, hyperinsulinemia or glucose intolerance, and hypertension. These conditions form the basis for Syndrome X (also called the metabolic syndrome). A sample of 52 non-Hispanic White mother-child pairs were compared with 92 Mexican-American mother-child pairs to assess the risk for abnormal lipid profiles, hyperinsulinemia, hypertension, and obesity (Reaven et al., 1998). The findings of this study showed higher levels of obesity and hyperinsulinemia in Mexican-American children and adults compared with non-Hispanic White children and adults and therefore indicated that the Mexican Americans had an increased risk for CVD. Subsequent recommendations for avoiding increased rates of Syndrome X in Mexican American populations included early dietary intervention and exercise modification (Reaven et al., 1998).

IMPACT ON SOCIAL AND EMOTIONAL HEALTH

In addition to the effects of obesity on physical health status and long-term chronic disease risk, obesity in childhood and adolescence can affect social and emotional well-being. As early as 5 years of age, higher weight status in girls was found to be associated with decreased body self-esteem and a perception of decreased cognitive abilities (Davidson and Birch, 2001). The same study found that independent of the girls' actual weight status, a higher level of parental concern about child obesity was associated with a lower perception of physical and cognitive abilities by the daughters.

Another study among kindergartners and first-graders found that obesity was associated with lower academic performance in unadjusted data; however, after social and economic variables (e.g., race and ethnicity as well as mothers' education levels) were considered, the association was no longer significant (Datar and Magnabosco, 2004). These findings suggest that obesity is a marker but not a causal factor in children's academic performance. However, this study points out that obesity is observed more easily by other students compared with SES characteristics, and its significant association (unadjusted) with lower academic performance can contribute to the stigma of obesity, even in the early years of elementary school. Mexican-American children may experience a double burden of stigmatization because of the combined effects of stigmas associated with both obesity and ethnic origin.

Obese children are often subject to teasing from their normal-weight peers. The degree of teasing has been associated with higher weight concerns, more loneliness, poorer self-perception of physical appearance, higher preference for sedentary and isolated activities, and lower preference for physical or social activities (Hayden-Wade et al., 2005). Obesity also can affect self-perceived quality of life. A study of 106 children and adolescents ages 5–18 years (60 percent of the youth were Mexican) who were referred to a children's hospital for evaluation of obesity found that the self-reported quality of life score of the obese children and youth was significantly lower than that of their normal-weight peers and was similar to the score reported by children diagnosed with cancer (Schwimmer et al., 2003). Another study of body image and adolescent mental health found that Hispanic girls were more depressed and had lower self-esteem than other racial and ethnic groups even after controlling for body image. This study concluded that Hispanic adolescents may be at increased risk for mental health problems (Siegel et al., 1999).

Mexican-American children and adolescents have had a long battle with obesity and continue to lead the nation with regard to the proportion of their population who are either obese or at high risk for becoming obese. In addition, they are exhibiting the co-morbidities associated with obesity. Mexican-American adults are demonstrating the poor health outcomes associated with obesity, including increased levels of diabetes and CVD. It is important to remember that today's adults were children and adolescents in the 1970s and 1980s when Mexican Americans were first recognized to be at a greater risk for obesity. Consequently, if Mexican-American adults currently have some of the highest rates of diabetes in the country, what will this population look like when the current group of children become adults?

Impact on Health Care Costs

Studies of health care expenditures in the United States have documented the high cost and sharp upward trend in expenditures attributable to obesity. Econometric models indicate that the annual cost of obesity-related health care is approximately $75 billion (expressed in 2003 dollars) and that approximately half of these expenditures are financed by public funds through Medicare and Medicaid programs (Finkelstein et al., 2004). Overall, per capita health care costs have been rising rapidly, from an estimated $2,188 per capita in 1987 to $3,298 per capita in 2001 (expressed in 2001 dollars). Approximately 27 percent of this increase, or $301 per capita, can be attributed to obesity-related health care costs (Thorpe et al., 2004).

Hospital discharge data indicate that the economic burden of obesity-related illness is also increasing among children and youth in the United States. From 1979 to 1999 discharges with a diagnosis of diabetes nearly doubled, obesity and gallbladder diseases tripled, and sleep apnea discharges increased fivefold (Wang and Dietz, 2002). The same study also documented a greater than threefold increase in obesity-associated hospital costs, from $35 million during 1979–1981 to $127 million during 1997–1999.

These studies did not identify specifically health care costs associated with increasing obesity in Mexican-American children and youth. However, since many Mexican-American families depend on publicly funded programs (such as Medicaid) for health care, and since many may be underinsured or uninsured, the high prevalence and rapid increase in obesity among Mexican Americans inevitably will place increasing demands on these health care providers and have important implications for the funding needs of these programs (Flores et al., 1998; Burgos et al., 2005).

To date no study has calculated the economic impact of obesity in Mexican-American children and youth. However, an analysis of the economic impact of obesity has been conducted for the state of California, where approximately 35 percent of the population is Mexican American, 50 percent of the infants born are Hispanic and primarily Mexican American, and a large immigrant (mainly Mexican) population exists. This analysis assessed the economic cost attributable to physical inactivity, being overweight, and obesity with respect to medical costs, workers compensation, and loss productivity. The results showed a $21.7 billion loss—$10.2 billion in medical care, $338 million in workers compensation, and $11.2 billion in loss productivity. The following annual costs were determined: physical inactivity, $13.3 billion; obesity, $6.4 billon; and being overweight, $2 billion. An increase to $28 billion by 2005 subsequently was forecast unless aggressive actions were taken (Chenoweth, 2005).

These data from California provide insight into the enormous economic costs associated with obesity. When these costs are projected to the national level in the United States and Mexico, the overall impact on health care costs is staggering. Moreover, the outlook is that these costs will continue to increase unless ways are found to prevent and control the adult and childhood obesity epidemic.

FACTORS INFLUENCING OBESITY IN MEXICAN-AMERICAN CHILDREN AND YOUTH

ENERGY BALANCE

Obesity is the end result of an energy imbalance, in which overall caloric intake exceeds caloric expenditure. The high and increasing levels of obesity in Mexican-American children and youth would suggest strongly that their energy intake exceeds their energy expenditure and that the imbalance has increased over time. This excess of energy intake over expenditure could be the result of changing dietary patterns favoring an increased intake of higher caloric foods, decreased energy expenditure through limited physical activity, or some combination of both effects.

A number of contextual factors also may influence energy balance. Cultural perceptions of children's ideal body physique by parents may influence child feeding patterns, favoring a robust physique early in life and thereby increasing a child's risk of obesity. Another potential contextual influence on energy balance is the generational status of the child's family, in other words, whether the child's family is the first or second or even a later generation living in the United States. Changes in energy balance in first-generation families may be affected by changes in types and quantity of food available after the families immigrate into the United States as well as by the process of acculturation in dietary preferences. Transition from traditional Mexican diets to American diets likewise may affect second and later generation families as succeeding generations become more acculturated. The insecure employment settings and the environment of poverty in which many Mexican Americans live also may have effects on energy balance by influencing dietary choices, physical activity opportunities, and access to health care.

Finally, it is possible that maternal factors, such as pre-pregnancy obesity, and genetic factors may influence obesity risk. A discussion on the potential impact of these factors on energy balance and obesity risk follows.

DIETARY PATTERNS AND OBESITY RISK

Data from national surveys indicate an overall increase in daily caloric intake, by approximately 150–200 calories, of American adults from 1971 to 2000 (CDC, 2004). The same trend appears to exist with regard to children—a recent IOM report found that "total calorie intake appears to have increased substantially over the past 25 years for preschool children and adolescent boys and girls, with more modest changes for children ages 6–11 years" (IOM, 2006). However, differences in caloric intake in relation to ethnicity were not defined.

Is the increased prevalence of obesity in Mexican-American children and youth related to the quality of their diets? Large scale dietary intake data to address this question were first provided in the HHANES. An analysis of food frequency demonstrated that Mexican-American children and youth reported eating from the recommended four food groups only 70 percent and 55 percent of the time, respectively (Murphy et al., 1990). Further analysis of these data by foreign-born as well as U.S.-born Mexican Americans demonstrates that foreign-born Mexican Americans reported eating fruits and vegetables more frequently and eating fewer sugars (NRC/IOM, 1999). Similar findings were seen in NHANES III in adolescents. Those adolescents living in less acculturated homes had less fat, protein, and energy in their diets and more folate (Mazur et al., 2003). Intakes of these nutrients increased with acculturation.

In a study of a nationally representative sample of children, dietary recall on two separate days was used to determine the frequency of fast-food intake. Hispanic children were the least likely to eat fast food as compared with non-Hispanic Whites and African Americans (Bowman et al., 2004). However, once gender, SES, and geographic region were controlled, Hispanic youth were similar in fast-food intake to non-Hispanic Whites. In a U.S. Department of Agriculture study, the diets of children and adolescents were examined using data from NHANES (1999–2000) and a healthy eating index, which measured 10 nutritional components, including the intake of recommended fruits and vegetables and of fat (Basiotis, 2004). This study showed that Mexican Americans overall have a better dietary intake profile than non-Hispanic Whites or Blacks. Furthermore, those born in Mexico had better intake profiles than those born in the United States.

Overall, dietary intake studies suggest that less acculturated children and adults have nutritionally better food intakes with respect to fruits and vegetables; however, as acculturation increases so does fat intake. Therefore, maintaining a traditional diet seems to be an important factor in preventing obesity in Mexican-American children and their families.

PHYSICAL ACTIVITY AND SEDENTARY BEHAVIORS

Physical activity is the second part of the obesity equation. Data from NHANES III on physical activity and television watching (Andersen et al., 1998) showed that Mexican-American boys and girls reported less physical activity (defined as engaging in three bouts of vigorous activity per week) than non-Hispanic White boys (80.2 percent versus 87.9 percent) and girls (72.6 percent versus 77.1 percent). Mexican-American boys and girls also reported watching more television than non-Hispanic Whites—33.3 percent versus 24.3 percent for boys and 28.3 percent versus 15.6 percent for girls watched more than four hours per day. Watching television is a sedentary activity and occupies time that might otherwise be devoted to more active pursuits. In addition, children are exposed to extensive advertising for high-calorie and low-nutrient foods and beverages (IOM, 2006). More research is needed to better define the television-watching habits of Hispanic and Latino children and youth and to determine how the content of Spanish- and English-language programming impacts their physical activity and dietary behaviors.

Data from the 2002 Youth Media Campaign Longitudinal Survey—a national survey on physical activity—showed that Mexican-American youth are significantly less likely to participate in organized sports than non-Hispanic Whites (25.9 percent versus 46.6 percent) and are somewhat less likely to report (within a seven-day period) participation in free-time play activity (74.6 percent versus 79.3 percent) (Duke et al., 2003). This survey also examined barriers to physical activity and found that Hispanic parents more frequently reported barriers related to transportation issues, a lack of appropriate facilities, expense, a lack of parent time, and a lack of neighborhood safety. However, neighborhood safety was the only barrier that was significantly increased for Hispanic parents when compared with the African-American and non-Hispanic White parents (41.2 percent versus 13.3 percent and 8.5 percent, respectively).

Other data on Hispanic adolescents show similar findings. The California Health Interview Survey 2003 found less regular physical activity among Hispanic (primarily Mexican American) than non-Hispanic White adolescents. Moreover, twice the percentage of Hispanic teens reported no physical activity when compared with non-Hispanic Whites (9.5 percent versus 4.1 percent) (Babey et al., 2005). Only 70 percent of Hispanic teens were in schools that required physical education. In those schools, Hispanic adolescents reported doing regular physical activity significantly more often than Hispanic adolescents in schools where physical education was not required (70.2 percent versus 58.6 percent). Overall, these studies suggest that Mexican-American children and youth are less engaged in regular physical activity than their non-Hispanic counterparts. Barriers to physical activity include the perception of unsafe neighborhoods, the cost (in dollars and time) of sport activities, and the lack of local recreational opportunities such as parks and open spaces. The latter is significant since soccer was reported as the most preferred sport of Hispanic teens in the 2002 Youth Media Campaign Longitudinal Survey.

CULTURALLY BASED PERCEPTIONS THAT INFLUENCE OBESITY

The perception of desirable body physique and what is considered "normal weight" can influence obesity risk by affecting dietary and physical activity behaviors. These perceptions have cultural overlays from current experience (e.g., from the fashion industry) and past experiences such as familial experiences with malnutrition or recurrent illness. These issues need to be explored with Mexican Americans, because they come from a complex cultural milieu involving both Mexican and American influences. Moreover, with a large proportion of immigrants recently arrived from Mexico and the majority of Mexican Americans maintaining some ties to the Latino culture, perceptions of normal weight for Mexican-American children, youth, and parents may be quite different from those of non-Hispanics.

Maynard et al. (2003) examined the NHANES III data to explore maternal perceptions of their children's weight status. Although only 65 percent of mothers identified their children as overweight when they had a BMI greater than the 95th percentile, there was no difference in this ability between Mexican-American and non-Hispanic White mothers (Maynard et al., 2003). However, using the same survey, Klaudt et al. (2002) found that Mexican-American mothers who rated their children as being at the correct weight or at a low weight had children with a higher BMI compared with non-Hispanic White mothers. This finding raises the possibility that Mexican-American mothers believe that a more rotund physique is normal. Even though the child might not be obese by BMI standards, if the mother's perception is that a "plump" child is healthy, then this perception will need to be addressed so that interventions to control obesity can be successful. Consequently, future research should seek to uncover a better understanding of what Mexican-American mothers consider to be good parenting practices with regard to diet and physical activity.

A more complete understanding of cultural perceptions regarding child rearing may need to involve educating not only the parents but also the entire extended family and community. Familism—the importance of family and culture—is a fundamental factor in Mexican-American families. Romero et al. (2004) hypothesized that this would be strongest in less-educated, Spanish-speaking, and poor families. Instead, the greater levels of familism were seen in those with more education, higher income, and bilingual or English-speaking families. Although this study involved a large, mobile immigrant population, it suggests that even with acculturation, Mexican Americans still retain a strong family orientation. As such, lifestyle changes for Mexican-American children probably will be achieved best by supporting changes at the family and community levels.

GENERATIONAL STATUS

Analyses of the HHANES data found that differences in height and weight among immigrant and U.S.-born Mexican-American children were primarily the result of parental SES, and that birthplace did not contribute significantly to either weight or height (NRC/IOM, 1999). Mexican-American children, whether U.S.- or non-U.S. born, had relatively normal weights during childhood compared to their heights. However, during adolescence there was more variability in weights between adolescent boys and girls, particularly with first-generation boys who demonstrated the lowest weights. In HHANES, 12–18-year-old adolescents showed increasing obesity in later generations. However, being foreign born did not demonstrate any difference in BMI for Mexican-American adolescents once age, gender, and SES were controlled (NRC/IOM, 1999). In another study that used data from the National Longitudinal Study of Adolescent Health, Hispanic adolescents born in the United States were twice as likely to be obese than those born outside of the country (Popkin and Udry, 1998). Mexican Americans were the largest Hispanic group in the sample and had the highest percentage (32 percent) over the 85th percentile (considered to be at-risk for obesity). Thus, these studies suggest that U.S.-born Mexican-American youth are more obese than those born in Mexico. This finding is consistent with recent data from the National Health Interview Survey indicating significantly higher rates of obesity and hypertension among U.S.-born Hispanic adults when compared with Hispanic immigrants residing in the United States for less than five years (CDC, 2006).

ACCULTURATION

Acculturation is the process of changing cultural customs, attitudes, perceptions, and behaviors. The time frame of the acculturation process varies from individual to individual and is driven by the living environment and other social pressures for acculturation, such as schools, friends, media, and work. Measures of acculturation usually assess changes in language usage, food preferences, leisure preferences, and social networks. The process of acculturation also can involve changes in perceptions and models of health and well-being that can have a major impact on an individual's health behaviors and assessments of health risk. Even though generational and immigrant status are linked closely to the acculturation process, they are not the same. For that reason, the effects of acculturation on Hispanic obesity need to be explored further.

In a study of immigrant Hispanic adults sampled from the National Health Interview Survey 1998, those who were in the United States for 15 years or longer had a greater likelihood of having a BMI of 30 or greater (Kaplan et al., 2004). Among Hispanics who had been in the United States fewer than 5 years, 9.4 percent had a BMI greater than 30; among those who had been in the United States for more than 15 years, 24.2 percent had a BMI greater than 30. In this study, Mexican Americans were more than 50 percent of the sample and had the highest proportion of obese adults.

In a study conducted in Washington State, Mexican immigrants were found to consume fewer fruits and vegetables as they became more acculturated (Neuhouser et al., 2004). Using data from NHANES III, Dixon et al. (2000) examined the differences in dietary intakes of adult Mexican-American men and women and found that those who were less acculturated took in less fat and more fiber and vitamins. Although these studies focused primarily on adults, they suggest that as immigrants become more acculturated, their diets change and obesity increases from one generation to the next. Since Mexican-American children and youth comprise such a large proportion of those living in immigrant families, the processes involved in acculturation may be major factors in the increasing prevalence of obesity.

WORKFORCE PARTICIPATION AND THE ENVIRONMENT OF POVERTY

Mexican Americans, who comprise two-thirds of all U.S. Hispanics, continue to be one of the poorest and youngest groups of Americans, with 37 percent of the populations under 18 years of age. The U.S. Census reports that 21.9 percent of Hispanic families live in poverty. In addition, even though Mexican Americans have a workforce participation equal to that of non-Hispanic Whites, they have the highest rate of being uninsured (BLS, 2004; DeNavas-Walt et al., 2005). Both parents typically are working to support their families, a situation that makes child care a major issue. This is particularly true for immigrant families who have higher rates of poverty (Burgos et al., 2005). In addition, with low levels of education, Mexican-American parents tend to have lower paying jobs that are less likely to provide insurance. Their jobs often have less security and typically less union protection, particularly for farm workers before their unionization. Thus, although Mexican Americans have high workforce participation, they continue to live in poverty without health insurance and with limited upward mobility. These realities will impact efforts to prevent obesity by limiting the availability of money to buy healthy food, live in safe areas, and have health insurance to receive preventive and therapeutic medical care.

Though many live in poverty, Mexican Americans are a heterogeneous population in many different ways: economically, culturally, educationally, and even regionally. The status of Mexican Americans currently is undergoing a dramatic change, which can be seen in states like California where Mexican Americans now hold leadership positions in government. This diversity in the population, from the poorest to the most powerful, needs to be considered in developing a strategic plan to improve the problem of obesity in this community while maintaining a focus on those most at risk and least able to help themselves.

MATERNAL AND GENETIC EFFECTS ON OBESITY RISK

Recent studies have suggested that maternal factors such as pre-pregnancy obesity may influence subsequent obesity risk for children, especially if born to a Hispanic mother (Whitaker, 2004; Salsberry and Reagan, 2005). Genetic factors that may influence energy usage through variable metabolic rates and the degree of fat storage are also potentially important. Preliminary studies in American–Pima Indian populations have shown genotypes in which metabolic rates are lower by as much as 150 Kcal/d, such that the unburned calories may increase the risk of obesity (Kovacs et al., 2005). The study's investigators were unable to show a direct association with obesity; however, further research may demonstrate a genetic risk for this population that would have significant implications for Mexican Americans who may share the same genotype. Thus, it is possible that Mexican and Mexican-American children with a high proportion of indigenous ancestry may have a greater tendency toward obesity.

CURRENT POLICIES AND PROGRAMS

Various intervention activities have been developed to address child obesity, including media-based health promotion, school-based interventions, community-level activities, health care and family counseling, and research and monitoring. Information on current intervention programs is available from a variety of sources (Action for Healthy Kids, 2005; International Life Sciences Institute, 2005; Shaping America's Youth, 2004). The majority of these interventions have addressed English-speaking audiences, but some programs and materials have been developed in Spanish.

Many current programs have been evaluated to assess their impact on obesity, and the results indicate that the programs have at least short-term reductions in obesity prevalence or improvements in obesity-related dietary and physical activity behaviors. However, these evaluations often are limited methodologically. For example, a recent review of school-based interventions by the Task Force on Community Preventive Services concluded that there was insufficient evidence to determine the effectiveness on children and adolescents of interventions in school settings (CDC, 2005c). Another recent report by the Preventative Services Task Force also cautioned that "interventions to treat overweight adolescents in clinical settings have not been shown to have clinically significant benefits and are not widely available" (Whitlock et al., 2005).

A wide variety of intervention activities that hold promise for successful outcomes are underway although their long-term effectiveness is still to be demonstrated. A number of these interventions have been adapted for use with Spanish-speaking children and families. As noted in the IOM report *Preventing Childhood Obesity: Health in the Balance*, it would be detrimental to wait for conclusive evidence before moving forward with interventions that, based on available evidence, are most likely to provide positive results (IOM, 2005).

This section provides an overview of current intervention activities in the media, schools, communities, and health care settings, as well as related research and monitoring activities. Primary attention is paid to policies and programs that are focused on or relevant to obesity prevention in Mexican-American or other Hispanic children and youth.

MEDIA-BASED HEALTH PROMOTION

The widespread access of Mexican-American families to Spanish media offers promising opportunities to provide health promotion information through media channels. The great majority of Mexican-American families have daily access to television, and radio continues to be a prominent media source for Latinos (Kissam et al., 2003). Access to the Internet is increasing rapidly. Studies by the Pew Internet and American Life Project found that half of all adult Hispanics who speak English had used the Internet and that 78 percent of those with Internet access are online at least 3–5 times a week (Spooner and Rainie, 2001). Although Mexican Americans have substantial media access, the quality of health information disseminated over these channels varies considerably in quality and consistency. Broadie et al. (1999) found that even though Latinos sought out information from the general media, they did not trust the media for health information and felt that media sources did not cover the health issues most relevant to minority communities.

Television viewing by Mexican-American children and youth may be particularly important as both a causal factor in obesity and as a potential source of intervention. A recent IOM report, *Food Marketing to Children and Youth: Threat or Opportunity*, found that children are being exposed to extensive advertising for high-calorie, low-nutrient foods but very limited advertising for more healthful foods and beverages (IOM, 2006). Information on the media exposure of "tweens" and "teens" is available, but there does not appear to be a current content analysis of food and beverage advertisements directed at Hispanic and Latino children and youth despite a high level of expenditure on Hispanic media and advertising (Roberts et al., 2005; Endicott et al., 2005).

Efforts are underway, however, to improve both the quantity and quality of health information content, although their effectiveness still needs to

be evaluated (Velez-Subervi, 1999). Descriptions of some of the more prominent Spanish-language media-based activities initiated by both government
and privately sponsored organizations follow. Additional Spanish-language
media activities are summarized in tabular form.

GOVERNMENT-SPONSORED MEDIA INTERVENTIONS

Government agencies in the United States and Mexico have initiated media-
based interventions to promote healthy eating and physical activity. Some of
these programs are briefly described below. Table C-2 summarizes information about these programs and provides information about several additional
government-sponsored media intervention activities.

TABLE C-2 Government-Sponsored Media Interventions

Program	Target Group	Program Description	Evaluation and Contact Information
VERB	"Tweens" (9–13 years)	— Social marketing campaign launched by CDC to promote physical activity. — Uses paid TV and radio advertising. — Website provides information and interactive games to motivate "tweens" and families to be physically active (http://www.verbnow.com/). — Includes health promotion content in Spanish on the CDC website.	— Based on formative research of attitudes and practices of youth relating to physical activity. — At one year, 74 percent of children aware of VERB. — Self-reported physical activity increased. Contact: http://www.cdc.gov/youthcampaign/research/resources.htm http://www.cdc.gov/spanish/VERB/Ninospercent20activos.htm
Eat Smart, Play Hard	6–18 years	—Website displays educational materials in Spanish for use in schools and community programs. — Materials include posters, activity workbooks, brochures, and bookmarks.	— Developed by the U.S. Department of Agriculture Contact: http://www.fns.usda.gov/eatsmartplayhard/Collection/sp-collect_tools.html

(Continued)

Todo en Sobrepeso y Obesidad	Older teens and adults	— Provides information on obesity and related cardiovascular risks for patients, health professionals, and families. — Content is culturally and linguistically adapted for use by Mexican Americans. — Related site, Todo en Diabetes, provides information for patients, professionals, and families concerned about diabetes.	Developed by Mexican Government Contact: http://www.todoensalud.org/Obesidad/jsp/intro_fam.jsp http://www.todoensalud.org/diabetes/jsp/Login.jsp
BAM	9–13 years	— Online site developed by CDC. — Provides information to help tweens make healthy behavioral choices.	Contact: http:www.bam.gov/site_terms.html
Powerful Bones, Powerful Girls	Tweens and teenage girls	— Online nutrition and physical activity site developed by CDC and the National Osteoporosis Foundation.	Contact: http://www.cdc.gov/powerfulbones
Small Steps/ Kids	Primary school age	— U.S. Department of Health and Human Services health promotion site for kids. — Links to adult site with Spanish content.	Contact: http://www.smallstep.gov/kids/index.cfm

VERB

The VERB campaign was developed by the Centers for Disease Control and Prevention (CDC) as a five-year social marketing campaign for "tweens," children of ages 9–13 years. The campaign is based on formative research that assessed youths' attitudes and practices relating to physical activity. Longitudinal evaluation of the campaign's impact demonstrated positive effects. Surveys conducted at baseline and at one year after the launch of the campaign found that 74 percent of the children surveyed were aware of the VERB campaign. Levels of self-reported, free-time physical activity increased among various subgroups of children aware of the campaign when compared with levels in children who were unaware of VERB (Huhman et al., 2005). Ongoing evaluation of the VERB campaign will provide valuable information on the potential effectiveness of Web-based health promotion. Though the VERB website for "tweens" does not have Spanish-language content, its images, games, and activities are designed to be appealing to all ethnic groups. VERB has health promotion information in Spanish on the CDC website, with links to a wide variety of health information.

Eat Smart, Play Hard

The U.S. Department of Agriculture (USDA) has also launched a national nutrition education and promotion campaign called Eat Smart, Play Hard, which was targeted at preschool and school-age children and their caregivers. The campaign uses multiple communication vehicles, approaches, and channels, including print materials and the Internet. In addition to English-language content, the campaign's website displays Spanish-language educational materials designed for use by children and adolescents in schools and community programs.

Todo en Sobrepeso y Obesidad

The Mexican government, in collaboration with professional societies and industry partners, has developed a health information website: Todo en Sobrepeso y Obesidad. The site provides information on obesity and related cardiovascular risks for patients, health professionals, and families. Because it originates in Mexico, the content is culturally and linguistically adapted for use by Mexican Americans. A related site, Todo en Diabetes, provides information specifically for patients, professionals, and families concerned about or caring for persons with diabetes.

PRIVATELY-SPONSORED MEDIA INTERVENTIONS

A variety of media-based interventions also have been privately sponsored. Some of the more prominent programs that provide Spanish-language content follow. These programs also are summarized in Table C-3, along with several additional privately supported media interventions.

Salud es Vida . . . Enterate!

Television and radio broadcasters have potential to reach a great number of Hispanics with health information. A prominent example is the health education initiative of Univision Communications Inc., Salud es Vida . . . Enterate! which was launched in 2003. This health promotion effort provides informational messages and programming—including public service announcements (PSAs), vignettes, news, and dedicated health programs featuring nationally recognized Hispanic celebrities and medical experts—on radio and television. To complement this effort, Univision.com has

TABLE C-3 Privately Sponsored Media Interventions

Program	Target Group	Program Description	Evaluation and Contact Information
Salud es Vida . . . Enterate!	Parents and older teens	— Sponsored by Univision. — Television and radio: Provides informational messages and programming on radio and television including PSAs, vignettes, news, and dedicated health programs. — Internet: Interactive website provides information on health issues and advice on healthful nutrition and physical activities. — Partners with Univision in this initiative include the Kaiser Family Foundation, the Ad Council, and many other health, community, and medical organizations.	— Impact evaluated based on calls to the Spanish-language call center of the American Diabetes Association. Contact: Univision Communications Inc. http://www.univision.com/content/channel.jhtml?chid=2&schid=8241 http://www.kff.org/entpartnerships/Univision-Announces-Year-Long-Health-Campaign-in-Partnership-With-the-Kaiser-Family-Foundation.cfm
Coalition for Healthy Children	Children, teens, and parents	— Involves marketers, media, nonprofits, foundations, and government agencies to provide consistent, research-based messages targeted to parents and children. — Coalition members incorporate messages into their communications activities. — Use of key messages to be reported by participating organizations to the Ad Council and shared with Coalition members via an online forum.	— Program impact to be measured by changes in attitudes and behavior of children and parents. — Results to be published and distributed to key constituencies. — No specific plans for translation into Spanish, but coalition members could address this need and share their efforts with others. Contact: http://healthychildren.adcouncil.org/about.asp

(Continued)

Program	Target Group	Program Description	Evaluation and Contact Information
Kidnetic	Primary school kids and teens	— Physical activity and nutrition promotion site developed by the International Food Information Council.	Contact: http://kidnetic.com/Whatis.aspx
Shaping America's Youth	All ages	— Online resource listing obesity programs. — Sponsors include Cadbury, Schweppes, Campbell Soup, FedEx, NIKE.	Contact: http://www.shapingamericasyouth.org/Default.aspx

developed a comprehensive Spanish-language website that provides information on a wide range of health issues and advice on healthful nutrition and physical activities. The campaign is not directed at children or adolescents, but the messages do reach Hispanic parents who are seeking information about nutrition, physical activity, and being overweight as those topics relate to caring for their children. Partners with Univision in this initiative include the Kaiser Family Foundation, the Ad Council, the American Diabetes Association, and many other health, community, and medical organizations.

COALITION FOR HEALTHY CHILDREN: COMBATING CHILDHOOD OBESITY

Another initiative to enhance health information for children and youth is the Coalition for Healthy Children, a public-private collaboration designed to use the collective strengths of marketers, the media, nonprofits, foundations, and government agencies to address the obesity crisis. With support from the Robert Wood Johnson Foundation and in cooperation with the Advertising Council, the coalition aims to provide consistent, research-based messages targeted at parents and children. The coalition's strategy is to have each of its members incorporate these common messages into their communications activities, including advertising, packaging, websites, grassroots programs, and marketing events. Program impact will be assessed through an ongoing tracking study. Although no specific plans have been developed for translating these or other messages into Spanish, coalition members could address this need and share their efforts with others.

SCHOOL-BASED INTERVENTIONS

A wide variety of school-based intervention programs have been developed but few are designed specifically for Hispanic children. However,

Spanish-language teaching materials are available from a number of sources, and many programs and policies that promote physical activity and provide or healthful food choices in schools can benefit all children, including Mexican Americans.

Implementing school-based obesity interventions can present a number of challenges (GAO, 2005). Changes in school curriculum to include more nutrition education or increased physical activity opportunities must be integrated into and contend with other academic priorities. Physical activity programs may be less controversial since changes in school food or vending policies must deal with the added costs of providing more healthful meals and possible lost income from vending contracts. School administrators cite a lack of program models and clear guidelines but at the same time want flexibility to adapt interventions to meet their local needs and resources.

Despite these challenges, many school-based interventions have been initiated (Food and Nutrition Service, 2005). Several intervention programs, including Bienestar and CATCH, have been undertaken and evaluated in schools with a high proportion of Mexican-American children. These intervention programs have combined nutrition education and have increased opportunities for physical activity with policy changes with regard to vending and the nutritional quality of school meals. These programs provide examples of promising strategies for school-based intervention that have been successful in schools with a high proportion of Mexican-American children. A complementary strategy, described below, is the development of school wellness policies as required by recent federal legislation.

BIENESTAR

Developed in San Antonio, Texas, Bienestar is a bilingual, nutrition and physical activity promotion program designed specifically for use in elementary schools with a high proportion of Hispanic children. The intervention is based on social cognitive theory that recognizes the need to change the social systems that influence children's behaviors. In line with this theoretical construct, the intervention consists of programs targeting parents, school health classes, cafeterias, and after-school programs.

The impact of the intervention on obesity and diabetes risk factors was evaluated, and the results were reported in a recent study in San Antonio, Texas (Trevino et al., 2005). This randomized, controlled trial found that after adjusting for covariates the mean fasting capillary glucose levels decreased in the intervention schools and increased in control schools. Fitness scores increased significantly in intervention children and decreased in control children. However, no significant difference was found in the percentage of body fat. Even though longer follow-up will be needed to determine long-term benefits, these results indicate the potential success of a multi-component, bilingual intervention to modify risk factors for diabetes.

CATCH

The Coordinated Approach to Child Health (CATCH) program in El Paso, Texas, implemented a school-based intervention to increase moderate to vigorous physical activity and to improve the nutritional content of school meals. Evaluation in 24 schools with a high proportion of Mexican-American children found that, for most intervention schools, the intervention was associated with significantly increased moderate to vigorous physical activity and decreased fat in school meals. However, some schools did not meet fat content goals, and no schools met the vigorous physical activity goals (Heath and Coleman, 2002). Other follow-up studies in a cohort of children from ethnically diverse backgrounds in California, Louisiana, Minnesota, and Texas have shown that behavioral changes associated with the CATCH intervention were maintained for three years without further intervention. Although not specific to any single ethnic group, these findings suggest that behavioral changes initiated during the elementary school years may persist into early adolescence (Nader et al., 1999).

WELLNESS POLICY DEVELOPMENT

An important policy development stemming from the Child Nutrition and WIC (Special Supplemental Nutrition Program for Women, Infants, and Children) Reauthorization Act of 2004 requires all school districts with a federally-funded school meals program to develop and implement wellness policies that address nutrition and physical activity by the start of the 2006–2007 school year. This new requirement for a defined wellness policy presents a significant opportunity for advancing school-based nutrition and physical activity promotion. School administrators, teachers, and parents should be encouraged to use the opportunity to review current policies and identify changes that can improve the healthfulness of the school environment and contribute to obesity prevention.

A number of resources are available to assist schools in developing wellness policies. The National Alliance for Nutrition and Activity has developed a set of model policies for use by local school districts. Resources to aid schools in formulating wellness policies include CDC's School Health Index, USDA's Changing the Scene guidelines, and Wellness Policy Development tools trainings from Action for Healthy Kids (Table C-4). Support for developing and implementing school wellness policies should be a high priority.

COMMUNITY-BASED INTERVENTIONS

Many community level interventions have been initiated to promote physical activity and nutrition improvement in children, adolescents, and adults. Examples of programs that specifically address the needs of Hispanic children and youth are described in the following sections as are more general programs that assist the community as a whole in implementing obesity prevention strategies. The programs cited are summarized in Table C-5.

TABLE C-4 School-Based Interventions and Teaching Materials

Program	Target Group	Program Description	Evaluation and Contact Information
Bienestar	Grades 3–5	— Bilingual instructional material. — Intervention based on social cognitive theory. — Programs target parents, school health classes, cafeterias, and after-school activities. — Primary objectives are to decrease dietary fat intake, increase fiber intake, increase physical fitness, and control body weight.	— Randomized controlled trial results show that intervention students have • Significantly increased dietary fiber intake, • Increased physical fitness levels, and • Decreased fasting capillary glucose levels. — However, no significant difference was found in the percentage of body fat in intervention and control children (Trevino et al., 2005). Contact: Social and Health Research Center http://www.sahrc.org/
CATCH (Coordinated Approach to Child Health)	Intervene grades K–5 Follow-up grades 6–8	Environmental Change Goals: — Reduce total fat, saturated fat, and sodium content of food served in school meals. — Increase the percent of physical education class time that students spend in moderate to vigorous physical activity to 40 percent. — CATCH Kids Club after School Program is available: http:www.flaghouse.com/afterSchool.asp	— Evaluation in 24 schools with a high proportion of Mexican-American children. — Intervention associated with significantly increased moderate to vigorous physical activity and decreased fat in school meals. — However, some schools did not meet fat content goals, and no schools met vigorous physical activity goals (Heath and Coleman, 2002). Contact: http://www.flaghouse.com/CatchPE.asp
School Wellness Policy Development	School staff and parents	— National Alliance for Nutrition and Activity (NANA) offers guidance on developing school wellness policies and lists resources from CDC and USDA. — Action for Healthy Kids also provides online guidelines.	Contact: http://www.schoolwellnesspolicies.org/ http://apps.need.cdc.gov/shi/default.aspxhttp://www.fns.usda.gov/tn/Healthy/changing.htmlhttp://www.actionforhealthykids.org/resources_wp.php

(Continued)

My Pyramid for Kids	Grades K–5	— Spanish version of USDA's "My Pyramid" food and physical activity guide.	Contact: http://teamnutrition.usda.gov/kids-pyramid.html
MiPirámide	Children and teens	— A Spanish-language version of MyPyramid.gov.MiPirámide: Pasos Hacia Una Mejor Salud, MyPyramid: Steps to a Healthier You emphasizes the same key messages as MyPyramid: • Making smart choices from every food group, • Finding a balance between food intake and physical activity, and • Getting the most nutrition from calories consumed.	— The MyPyramid graphics, website, and handouts and other materials have been translated into Spanish. These resources can be accessed at http://www.MyPyramid.gov.
What's to Eat	Parents and older children	— Spanish version of a video to assist families prepare and enjoy healthy food. — Stanford Health Promotion Resource Center	Contact: http://hprc.stanford.edu/pages/store/catalog.asp?Spanish
Learning Zone Express	Grades K–12	— Posters and teaching aids in Spanish. — Online store and resource center.	Contact: http://www.learningzoneexpress.com

GOVERNMENT-SPONSORED INTERVENTIONS

DIVIÉRTASE Y SEA ACTIVO

Diviértase y Sea Activo (Have Fun and Be Active) is the title of a physical activity program funded by the Contra Costa Children and Families Commission of Contra Costa County, California. A video, available in Spanish and English, encourages families to choose a healthy, active lifestyle by showing images of families participating in a variety of physical activities. A related activity also provided by the Commission is the scheduling of community health promotion fairs for Hispanic families; the fairs are advertised to the community as Diviértase y Manténgase Saludable Talleres (Have Fun and Be Healthy Workshops). At these events families learn to prepare healthy snacks, play games, and participate in fun physical activities. This program provides an interesting model in which activities potentially contributing to obesity prevention can be integrated into a larger framework of community efforts to promote child health.

TABLE C-5 Government-Sponsored Interventions

Program	Target Group	Program Description	Evaluation and Contact Information
Diviértase y Sea Activo	1–5 years	— An initiative of the Contra Costa Children and Families Commission that includes the following: • Video, in Spanish, showing families being physically active with children ages 1–5 years. • Community health promotion fairs for Hispanic families	Contact for purchase of the video: http://www.abridgeclub.com/Videos_&_DVD.htm#Have%20Fun%20&%20Be%20Active Brochure for health fair: http://www.cchealth.org/espanol/pdf/wic_funshops_esp._2005_10.pdf
California Latino 5-a-Day		— Promotes fruit and vegetable consumption among Spanish-speaking adults. — Designed to reach Latinos in their homes and communities. — Has developed Children's 5-a-Day Power Play Campaign targeted to 9–11-year-old children. — Not in Spanish but designed to appeal to Latino children who speak English.	— Evaluation by telephone interviews found an increase in fruit and vegetable consumption and increased awareness of the 5-a-Day message among Spanish-speakers. — Not addressing children and adolescents directly, but may have impact by modifying parents' attitudes and food purchases. Contact: http://www.dhs.ca.gov/ps.cdic/cpns/lat5a-day/lat_research.htm
Food Stamp Program		— Assists low-income families in buying nutritious foods. — Eligibility based on income; all children born in the United States are entitled to the benefits. — However, many eligible Latinos do not participate in the program.	Contact: http://www.sfgate.com/cgi-bin/article.cgi?file=/chronicle/archive/2004/10/01/BAGG691K4B1.DTL

CALIFORNIA LATINO 5-A-DAY

California's Latino 5-a-Day program promotes fruit and vegetable consumption among Spanish-speaking adults. The intervention is designed to reach Latinos in their homes, where they shop, where they eat, and where they gather with other community members. Evaluation of the program's impact by telephone interviews found a significant increase in fruit and vegetable consumption and increased awareness of the 5-a-Day message among Spanish-speakers in the target area of the campaign. Although the program does not directly address children and adolescents, the campaign may have an impact by modifying parent's attitudes and food purchase behaviors. California also has developed a Children's 5-a-Day Power Play Campaign targeted to 9–11-year-old children. Even though the program is not presented in Spanish, it is designed to appeal to English-speaking Latino children.

FOOD STAMP PROGRAM

Participation in the food stamp program can assist low-income families in buying nutritious foods that may be less likely to contribute to obesity. Eligibility for food stamps is based on income, and all children born in the United States are entitled to the benefits. However, a survey by the Alameda County Community Food Bank estimated that 1.7 million Californians, many of them Latino, are eligible for food stamps but do not participate in the program. These findings suggest that an educational campaign to expand awareness of and participation in the food stamp program by Mexican Americans could help improve access to healthful foods and would be a valuable component of an overall obesity prevention strategy.

PRIVATE AND COMMUNITY-SPONSORED INTERVENTIONS

Many promising community-based programs have been initiated by private and non-profit organizations that are concerned with the health and welfare of children. Examples of such programs are described in the following sections and summarized in Table C-6.

CANFit

The California Adolescent Nutrition and Fitness (CANFit) Program is designed to help communities build the capacity to improve the nutrition and physical activity status of low-income ethnic youth who are 10–14 years old. CANFit has launched health promotion campaigns specifically addressing the Hispanic community. For example, the Adelante con Leche Semi-descremada 1 percent campaign, implemented in Los Angeles in 1999–2000, was designed to motivate Latino youth and their families to switch from drinking whole or two-percent milk, to drinking one-percent or fat-free milk. Based on sales report data, the Adelante campaign resulted in a 200 percent increase in one-percent milk sales (see Table C-6 for reference).

LATINO HEALTH ACCESS

Latino Health Access is a community-based health promotion program that uses community health promoters who are recruited to work in the communities where they live. The *promotores* are skilled at educating and serving as role models for their peers. The Children and Youth Initiative, a program of Latino Health Access in California, is a school- and community-based intervention that is designed specifically for assisting children who live in high-risk environments to adopt nutrition, physical activity, and other positive behaviors that promote good health.

TABLE C-6 Private and Community-Sponsored Interventions

Program	Target Group	Program Description	Evaluation and Contact Information
CANFit (California Adolescent Nutrition and Fitness program)	10–14 years	— Provides training and technical assistance to youth-serving organizations. — Develops educational materials and social marketing programs. — Advocates for policies that enhance nutrition and physical activity. — Awards academic scholarships. — Funds innovative community-based projects. — CANFit is funded by private donations.	— Example program: The *Adelante con Leche Semidescremada 1 percent* campaign. — Promoted switching to one-percent or fat-free milk. — Used paid Hispanic radio, print advertising, and television; one-percent milk tastings. — Resulted in a 200 percent increase in one-percent milk sales. Contact: http://www.canfit.org/programs.html
Latino Health Access	Children and youth	— Uses community health promoters to work in the communities where they live. — *Promotores* are skilled at educating and serving as role models for their peers. — The Children and Youth Initiative assists children in high-risk environments to adopt healthful nutrition and physical activity and other positive behaviors that promote good health.	Contact: http://www.latinohealthaccess.org/aboutus.shtml

(Continued)

Kraft Salsa, Sabor y Salud	Latino families	— An eight-session healthy-lifestyle course for Latino families to reduce risks for obesity and related health problems. — Since 2003, the program has reached nearly 10,000 adults and children in 50 community organizations in six states.	Contact: http://www.kraft.com/responsibility/nhw_communitybased.aspx
Latino Nutrition Coalition	Latino families	— A consortium of industry, scientists and chefs in collaboration with the Oldways Preservation Trust. — Promotes programs in food stores, schools, restaurants, and clinics and sponsors community events.	Contact: http://www.latinonutrition.org/http://oldwayspt.org/index.php?area=latino_nutrition_coalition

SALSA, SABOR Y SALUD

Kraft has partnered with the National Latino Children's Institute to develop Salsa, Sabor y Salud (Food, Fun, and Fitness), an eight-session healthy-life-style course for Latino families. The program supports Hispanic families in adopting healthy lifestyles that will reduce the risk of obesity and related health problems. Launched in 2003, Salsa, Sabor y Salud has reached nearly 10,000 adults and children through 50 community organizations in six states.

LATINO NUTRITION COALITION

The Latino Nutrition Coalition is a consortium of industry leaders, scientists, and chefs in cooperation with the Oldways Preservation Trust to promote better Latino health through traditional foods and lifestyles. The Coalition will focus on practical programs of education and promotion in grocery stores, schools, health clinics, and restaurants. Initiatives that will include community fiestas and festivals are planned in five or six cities.

HEALTH CARE INTERVENTIONS

Mexican Americans and other Hispanics face a number of barriers in accessing health care, including language barriers, cultural differences, poverty, lack of health insurance, and transportation difficulties. These challenges complicate the provision of health care interventions to prevent and manage obesity in Mexican-American children. Evaluation of interventions in the health care setting has encountered methodological limitations. In 2002 the U.S. Preventive Services Task Force concluded that "the evidence is insufficient to recommend for or against behavioral counseling in primary care settings to promote physical activity," noting that there were no completed trials with children or adolescents that compared counseling with usual care practices (USPSTF, 2002). In 2003 another task force report concluded that "the evidence is insufficient to recommend for or against routine behavioral counseling to promote a healthy diet in unselected patients in primary care settings," noting that "no controlled trials of routine behavioral dietary counseling for children or adolescents in the primary care setting were identified" (USPSTF, 2003). As noted previously, a recent task force report cautioned that "interventions to treat overweight adolescents in clinical settings have not been shown to have clinically significant benefits and are not widely available." Although much more needs to be done to provide a more adequate research base, both government-sponsored and privately supported efforts are underway to address obesity in clinical settings. Examples of health care interventions that address Hispanic populations are highlighted in the following sections and are summarized in Table C-7.

TABLE C-7 Government-Supported and Privately Sponsored Health Care Interventions

Program	Target Group	Program Description	Evaluation and Contact Information
Vida Saludable, Corazon Contento	Women 40–64 years	— Translated and adapted from the WISEWOMAN CVD prevention program funded by CDC. — Offers guidance to health care providers in screening for CVD risk factors, lifestyle counseling to improve diet and physical activity, and clinical referral and follow-up services. — Support provided to Spanish-speaking women to promote healthy diet and physical activity within their families.	— The three-session intervention emphasizes readiness for change, goal-setting, individual tailoring, self-monitoring, and social support. — Counseling is facilitated by bilingual community health workers. — California is currently planning to pilot test the guide in five sites. Contact: http://www.hpdp.unc.edu/wisewoman/vida.htm http://wwwtest.cdc.gov/wisewoman/project_locations/california.htm

(Continued)

WIC Program	Birth to 5 years	— The WIC program serves 8 million women, infants, and children, almost half of United States' infants and a quarter of children 1–5 years of age. — In 2002, for the first time, Hispanics made up the largest group of WIC participants (38.1). — In California, 70 percent of WIC participants are Latino. — The WIC program is a major point of contact of Latinos with health care professionals.	Contact: http://www.fns.usda.gov/oane/MENU/Published/WIC/FILES/PC2002.htm
Kidshape	6–14 years and parents	— Offered in Spanish or English. — Eight weekly classes, two hours each. — Parents and children must attend. — Classes focus on healthy eating, behavior change principles, and physical activity.	— Website reports that: • 87 percent lose weight. • 80 percent report sustained weight loss at 1.5–2.5 year follow-up. Contact: http://www.cchealth.org/espanol/detalles_sobre_kidshape.html http://www.kidshape.com/Pages/programs.htm

GOVERNMENT-SUPPORTED HEALTH CARE INTERVENTIONS

Vida Saludable, Corazon Contento

The *Vida Saludable, Corazon Contento* guide is translated and adapted from the WISEWOMAN CVD prevention program for underserved and underinsured women ages 40 to 64 years. Funded by CDC, this program offers guidance to health care providers on screening for CVD risk factors, lifestyle counseling to improve diet and physical activity, and clinical referral and follow-up services. The program involves a three-session intervention that emphasizes readiness for change, goal-setting, individual tailoring, self-monitoring, and social support. Counseling is facilitated by bilingual community health workers. Although not designed to reach children and adolescents directly, the information and support provided to Spanish-speaking women potentially can assist in promoting healthy dietary and physical activity practices within their families. California currently is planning to pilot test the guide in five sites.

WIC Program

The WIC program serves 8 million women, infants, and children—almost half of the United States' infants and a quarter of 1–5 year olds. In 2002, for the first time, Hispanics made up the largest group of WIC participants (38.1 percent) (Table C-7). In states with a high proportion of Latinos, the great majority of WIC participants are Latino. For example, in California, 70 percent of WIC participants are Latino. This high level of participation makes the WIC program a major point of contact for Latinos with health care professionals and an important potential source of counseling with regard to a healthful diet and physical activity. At the same time, the limitations of the WIC program are clear: the program provides only limited health counseling on an infrequent basis. Such minimal exposure and follow-up is unlikely to be adequate to substantially affect behaviors.

PRIVATELY SPONSORED HEALTHCARE INTERVENTIONS

The Kidshape family lifestyle intervention is designed to promote healthful dietary and physical activity behaviors in 6–14-year-old overweight children and their parents. This clinical intervention has been implemented in various locations in southern California. The program is now being implemented in both English and Spanish in a clinic in northern California (Contra Costa County) as part of a larger community-based effort to prevent and treat childhood obesity in a population with a high proportion of Mexican Americans. The eight-week program is family-oriented and requires that both parents and children attend all of the weekly sessions. It is reported that 87 percent of children lose weight and 80 percent maintain weight loss 1.5–2.5 years after finishing the program, but the Kidshape website does not provide the supporting data (Table C-7). While clearly needing evaluation, the Kidshape program is an example of the type of family-based clinical intervention that seems most promising.

RESEARCH AND MONITORING

Research and monitoring activities are a critical part of the overall strategy to prevent child obesity. As noted above, there are intrinsic challenges in conducting evaluations of school-based and community intervention programs. Continuing and expanded research is needed to define best practices and demonstrate effectiveness. Ongoing monitoring of weight status and behavioral trends also is needed to gauge long-term progress in obesity prevention.

NATIONAL-LEVEL SURVEY AND MONITORING ACTIVITIES

At the national level in the United States, the ongoing Health and Nutrition Examination surveys, Behavioral Risk Factor Surveillance surveys, and Youth Risk Behavior surveys provide essential information on obesity prevalence and behavioral trends. However, data from these sources may not be specific or detailed enough to characterize and monitor the attitudes and behaviors of children and youth with regard to dietary and physical activity behaviors. To address this need, CDC has developed the Youth Media Campaign Longitudinal Survey (YMCLS), an annual national telephone survey of young people ages 9–13 years and their parents. The YMCLS is designed to measure the physical activity–related beliefs, attitudes, and behaviors of youth and their parents and to monitor youth exposure to the VERB social marketing campaign. Survey results provide information on the VERB campaign's impact and guide the campaign's evolution.

The surveys also provide a valuable research base that can aid in the design of other obesity prevention efforts. More specifically, focused interviews with Hispanic teens and parents documented a variety of cultural attitudes that may affect the adoption of healthful physical activity behaviors (Table C-8). For example, Hispanic youth are encouraged to put family needs above their own, and activity for personal benefit may be discouraged. Household chores and baby-sitting younger siblings after school while parents work were identified as barriers, especially for girls. Physical activity was considered as merely playing and a distraction, and no connection was seen between physical activity and health benefits. Parents were reluctant to involve their kids in programs that didn't seem culturally relevant or that were not sanctioned by cultural authority figures they trust. These data indicate the very useful information obtainable by telephone surveys and supplemental interviews with Hispanic respondents.

STATE-LEVEL SURVEY ACTIVITIES

National data from the sources described previously often are inadequate to assess the status of state populations or specific subgroups that may vary substantially from overall national trends. State- and population-specific surveys frequently are needed to sufficiently assess obesity prevalence and the attitudes and behaviors related to obesity risk. Several California state-level surveillance and monitoring programs that may serve as useful examples are summarized in Table C-8. In particular, the California Health Interview Survey (CHIS)—conducted in English, Spanish, Chinese, Korean, and Vietnamese—is perhaps the nation's most culturally inclusive survey. The CHIS has been used to report on several factors relating to childhood obesity, including dietary intakes, physical activity, and environmental issues contributing to obesity.

ONLINE FORMATIVE RESEARCH

For Mexican-American parents and youth, having access to the Internet offers the potential to do online research that can reach thousands of respondents. Data provided online are already in electronic form and are ready to be tabulated and analyzed statistically. Respondents provide demographic information such as age, gender, place of residence, income, and education level for use in interpreting the information. Longitudinal follow-up is feasible via e-mail to assess response to an intervention. Research and monitoring using

TABLE C-8 Research and Monitoring Activities

Program	Target Group	Program Description	Evaluation and Contact Information
Youth Media Campaign Longitudinal Survey	9–13 years	— Annual national telephone survey of young people ages 9–13 years and their parents. — Conducted by CDC. — Measures physical activity-related beliefs, attitudes, and behaviors of youth and their parents. — Monitors youth exposure to the VERB campaign. — Evaluates the VERB campaign's impact. — Supplemental interviews with Hispanics provided culture-specific insights.	Contact: http://www.cdc.gov./youthcampaign/research/PDF/4.4.10-HisLatExSummaryRes.pdf
Children's Healthy Eating and Exercise Practices Survey	9–11 years	— Designed to assess dietary and physical activity patterns in children 9–11 years. — Sample of children from 2000 households included 38 percent Latino.	— California Department of Health Services. Contact: http://www.dhs.ca.gov/ps/cdic/cpns/research/calcheeps2003.html
Teen Eating, Exercise, and Nutrition Survey	12–17 years	— Provides information on teen dietary and exercise behaviors in 1998. — Assesses differences in behaviors in relation to age and gender.	Contact: http://www.dhs.ca/gov/ps.cdic/cpns/research/calteens2000.html
High School Fast Food Survey		— Conducted in 2003. — Survey examined school food service practices in a sample of California high schools.	— Public Health Institute, 2003. Contact: http://www.phi.org/pdf-library/fastfoodsurvey2000.pdf
California Health Interview Survey	1–18 years	— Conducted in 2001, 2003, 2005 by random dialed telephone survey in multiple languages. — Direct data from adolescents and for children from most knowledgeable adults.	— UCLA Center for Health Policy, School of Public Health Contact: http://www.chis.ucla.edu/default.asp

the Internet should be explored as a promising option for future development and evaluation of obesity prevention efforts.

THEORETICAL FRAMEWORK FOR INTERVENTION

Although interventions to treat obesity in children and adolescents who are already overweight can be successful, the process often requires intensive and sustained intervention, and long-term success is not assured. Moreover, Mexican-American children have limited access to health care, and costs, language, and other barriers can be significant. These realities underscore the conclusion of the IOM report *Preventing Obesity: Health in the Balance* that the strategy to address childhood obesity must be to focus on primary prevention (IOM, 2005).

A recent series of meetings coordinated by the Berkeley Media Studies Group looked at ways to accelerate the development of effective policies to foster healthier nutrition and eating environments. The "acceleration" meetings reviewed the experience of other public health prevention efforts such as those addressing tobacco, alcohol, firearms, and traffic safety. The summary of these meetings suggested that based on the experience of these other public health efforts, the path of least resistance for obesity prevention would be to focus on individual behavior change (Dorfman et al., 2005). This strategy puts the onus of responsibility on individuals to adopt healthful nutrition and physical activity habits. However, individual behavior change is unlikely to be successful unless positive behavioral changes are supported by the media, school, community, and health care environments in which individuals live.

The discussions at the acceleration meetings led to the conclusion that prevention efforts must shift focus from behavior to policy changes that affect the environments where behaviors take place. Although policy changes are more likely to meet more resistance than interventions that focus on individual behavior change, a policy change strategy offers the best opportunity to achieve effective and sustained prevention.

BEHAVIORAL THEORY

The theoretical framework described in the IOM report *Preventing Obesity: Health in the Balance* used an ecological systems theory model that depicts the behavioral settings and leverage points that influence food intake and energy expenditure (IOM, 2005). The child or adolescent is seen as being at the center of concentric rings of influence from family, school, community, industry, and government, and the larger culture and society. Leverage points that influence behavior include the food system, opportunities for physical activity or sedentary behavior, and information regarding the health implications of dietary behaviors and physical activity. Behavioral choices within this ecological system also are seen as affected by social norms and values.

Another behavioral theory that has been used in conceptualizing strategies for obesity prevention is social learning theory. This theory emphasizes the importance of observing and modeling the behaviors, attitudes, and emotional reactions of others. In this model, developed principally by Bandura, most human behavior is learned through observation and modeling. The social learning theory model, later renamed by Bandura as social cognitive theory, was used in developing the multicomponent, school-based Bienestar intervention (Bandura, 1986; Trevino et al., 1998). According to this model, social systems in the individual's environment, in addition to internal standards and self-evaluation, mediate the relationship between the individual's knowledge and his or her consequent behaviors. Because of the importance of social systems in the individual's environment, the Bienestar program designed components that affected the child's environment in the classroom, cafeteria, after school, and home settings. Another intervention focusing on increasing fruit and vegetable consumption also used social learning theory by emphasizing changes in the home environment and parental support to achieve positive behavioral changes in 10–12-year-old children (Gribble et al., 2003).

The ecological systems model and the social cognitive theory model both appear to be valid constructs for the development of obesity prevention interventions, since both recognize the importance of environmental factors in influencing behaviors. However, an issue to be considered in using either model is whether Mexican-American families have the same level of empowerment as non-Hispanic families to make changes in schools and community environments. Mexican Americans may be more fatalistic about health or about their ability to make changes. Given these concerns, it is unclear that there currently exists a best practice model for obesity prevention in Mexican-American children. Further research is needed to clarify the kinds of intervention strategies that will work best in Hispanic communities.

EVIDENCE-BASED APPROACH

The IOM report describes the need for an evidence-based approach to the development of obesity prevention interventions by using multiple sources of evidence, including randomized controlled trials (if available), quasi-experimental, and observational studies. It is critical to systematically evaluate the effectiveness of intervention efforts, while at the same time to recognize the practical realities and the fiscal and socio-political environments in which programs are implemented. Because of these constraints, research has evaluated only a limited number of interventions relevant to obesity prevention in Mexican-American children. Additional research is needed to define best practice models in media, school, community, and health care settings. Attention should be focused on the development and testing of community empowerment models and on interventions that draw on and incorporate values and beliefs stemming from Mexican culture, music, art, and literature.

RECOMMENDATIONS FOR ACTION

Overall goals for obesity prevention in Mexican-American children parallel those for all children and youth as expressed in IOM's *Preventing Obesity: Health in the Balance*. In the long term, the overriding goals are to achieve a reduction in the incidence and prevalence of obesity; improve dietary patterns to be consistent with dietary guidelines; meet physical activity guidelines; and achieve physical, psychological, and cognitive growth and development goals. However, more specific intermediate goals and recommendations that address the specific needs of Mexican-American children and youth must be defined.

Achieving policy, environmental, and behavioral goals for obesity prevention for Mexican-American children and youth will require interventions at many levels, including television, print, and electronic media; schools; communities; and health care settings. To be successful, these efforts must be supported by ongoing research and monitoring and by effective advocacy.

Some key issues to be addressed include the following: (a) the need for comprehensive, multifaceted interventions that can address dietary and physical activity behaviors; (b) greater insight into the feasibility of scaling up interventions to programs in large population groups; and (c) an increased understanding of ways to sustain interventions after initial start-up funds are no longer available. Outlined below are a variety of potential actions that might be recommended and prioritized.

MEDIA-BASED INTERVENTIONS

Media-based interventions are appealing because of their potential to reach large target audiences and for their low cost. Given the high level of access that Mexican-American families have to television and radio as well as the growing access they have to the Internet, especially by older children and youth, these media channels are an increasingly important means of providing information and motivation for healthy lifestyle choices. Another appealing feature of media-based interventions is the ability of electronic content to be shared internationally, in particular between Mexico and the Mexican-American populations in the United States. At the same time, food and beverage advertising through the same media can promote consumption of high-calorie and low-nutrient food and beverages and can negatively influence dietary and physical activity behaviors, thus increasing the risk of obesity. Specific actions that support expanding the potential and reducing the negative impact of media-based messages are cited in the following list.

HEALTH INFORMATION IN TELEVISION, RADIO, AND PRINT MEDIA

- Establish policies and guidelines that define appropriate marketing of foods and beverages to children and youth in general and specifically to Mexican-American children and youth.
- Increase the number of new industry products and advertising messages that promote energy balance at a healthy weight and are targeted to Mexican-American consumers.

- Develop culturally appropriate Web content that specifically targets Mexican-American children, youth, and parents.
- Develop Web content in Spanish, or adapt it from existing English language websites, to provide accurate and appealing health information and to offer tips and guidance in choosing healthy lifestyles.

SCHOOL-BASED INTERVENTIONS

School environments provide an important influence on children's behaviors and can foster healthful nutrition and physical activity or negatively influence these behaviors. Many of the interventions currently being implemented and evaluated are carried out in the school setting. Some key strategies for fostering health-promoting school environments include the following:

- Provide training for and support development of school wellness policies that promote healthful school nutrition and physical activity environments.
- Implement school food service and vending policies that encourage healthful dietary choices.
- Support the development and dissemination of language and culturally appropriate health education materials for Mexican-American children and youth.
- Support research to develop and evaluate school-based interventions that are sustainable and effective in promoting increased participation in healthful physical activity.

COMMUNITY-BASED INTERVENTIONS

Community-based youth programs and policies that create environments where children, youth, and families can share physical activity are critical components of an obesity prevention strategy.

- Support expansion of community-based youth programs that serve Mexican-American children and youth.
- In neighborhoods with a high proportion of Hispanic families, support policies such as the expansion of park facilities, sidewalks, and bike paths that encourage safe physical activity.

NOTE

1. The metabolic syndrome is diagnosed when an individual has at least three of five metabolic abnormalities: glucose intolerance, abdominal obesity, elevated triglyceride levels, low high-density lipoprotein levels, and high blood pressure. TABLE C-3 Privately Sponsored Media Interventions

REFERENCES CITED

Action for Healthy Kids. 2005. *Events, Programs, and Reports*. [Online]. Available: http://www.actionforhealthykids.org [accessed April 15, 2006].

Agredano Y, Schetzina K, Mendoza F. 2004. Are immigrant Mexican-American children at greater risk for asthma? *Pediatric Research* 1326.

Andersen R, Crespo C, Bartlett S, Cheskin L, Pratt M. 1998. Relationship of physical activity and television watching with body weight and level of fatness among children. *Journal of the American Medical Association* 279(12):938–942.

Babey S, Diamant A, Brown R, Hastert T. 2005. *California Adolescents Increasingly Inactive*. Los Angeles: UCLA Center for Health Policy Research.

Bandura A. 1977. *Social Learning Theory*. Englewood Cliffs, NJ: Prentice Hall.

Bandura A. 1986. *Social Foundations of Thought and Action: A Social Cognitive Theory*. Englewood Cliffs, NJ: Prentice Hall.

Basiotis P, Carlson A, Gerrior S, Juan W, Lino M. 2004. The Healthy Eating Index, 1999–2000: Charting dietary patterns of Americans. *Family Economics and Nutrition Review* 16(1):39–48.

BLS (Bureau of Labor Statistics). 2004. *Comparison of Labor Force Participation Rates and the Age of Composition of Hispanic and White Non-Hispanic Men. Employment Projections*. Washington, DC: U.S. Department of Labor.

Bowman SA, Gortmaker SL, Ebbeling CB, Pereira MA, Ludwig DS. 2004. Effect of fast-food consumption on energy intake and diet quality among children in a national household survey. *Pediatrics* 113(1):112–118.

Broadie M, Kjellson N, Hoff T, Parker M. 1999. Perception of Latinos, African Americans, and Whites on media as a health information source. *Howard Journal of Communication* 10(3):147–167.

Burgos A, Schetzina K, Dixon B, Mendoza F. 2005. Importance of generational status in examining access to and utilization of health care services by Mexican-American children. *Pediatrics* 115(3):e322–e330.

CDC (Centers for Disease Control and Prevention). 2003. Prevalence of diabetes and impaired fasting glucose in adults—United States, 1999–2000. *Morbidity and Mortality Weekly Report* 52(35):833–837.

CDC. 2004. Trends in intake of energy and macronutrients—United States, 1971–2000. *Morbidity and Mortality Weekly Report* 53(4):80–82.

CDC. 2005a. *National Diabetes Fact Sheet*. [Online]. Available: http://www.diabetes.org/uedocuments/NationalDiabetesFactSheetRev.pdf [accessed November 10, 2006].

CDC. 2005b. *Prevalence of Overweight Among Children and Adolescents: United States 1999–2002*. [Online]. Available: http://www.cdc.gov/nchs/products/pubs/pubd/hestats/overwght99.htm. [accessed November 10, 2006].

CDC. 2005c. Public health strategies for preventing and controlling overweight and obesity in school and worksite settings: A report on recommendations of the Task Force on Community Preventive Services. *Morbidity and Mortality Weekly Report* 54(10):1–12. [Online]. Available: http://www.cdc.gov/MMWR/preview/mmwrhtml/rr5410a1.htm [accessed November 10, 2006].

CDC. 2006. *Physical and Mental Health Characteristics of U.S. and Foreign-Born Adults: United States, 1998–2003*. Advance Data from vital and health statistics No. 369. Hyattsville, MD: National Center for Health Statistics.

Chenoweth D. 2005. *The Economic Cost of Physical Inactivity, Obesity, and Overweight in California Adults: Health Care, Workers Compensation, and Loss Productivity*. New Bern, NC: Chenoweth and Associates, Inc.

Cole TJ, Bellizzi MC, Flegal KM, Dietz WH. 2000. Establishing a standard definition for child overweight and obesity worldwide: International Survey. *British Medical Journal* 320(7244):1240–1243.

Cruz ML, Weigensberg MJ, Huang TT, Ball G, Shaibi GQ, Goran MI. 2004. The metabolic syndrome in overweight Hispanic youth and the role of insulin sensitivity. *Journal of Clinical Endocrinology and Metabolism* 89(1):108–113.

Daniels SR, Khoury PR, Morrison JA. 1997. The utility of body mass index as a measure of body fatness in children and adolescents: Differences by race and gender. *Pediatrics* 99(6):804–807.

Datar A, Magnabosco JL. 2004. Childhood overweight and academic performance: National study of kindergartners and first-graders. *Obesity Research* 12(1):58–68.

Davidson KK, Birch LL. 2001. Weight status, parental reaction and self-concept in five-year-old girls. *Pediatrics* 107(1):46–53.

del Rio-Navarro BE, Velazquez-Monroy O, Sanchez-Castillo CP, Lara-Esqueda A, Berber A, Fanghanel G, Violante R, Tapia-Conyer R, James W. 2004. The high prevalence of overweight and obesity in Mexican children. *Obesity Research* 12(2):215–223.

DeNavas-Walt C, Proctor B, Lee C. 2005. *Income, Poverty, and Health Insurance Coverage in the United States: 2004.* U.S. Census Bureau. Washington, DC: U.S. Department of Commerce.

Dixon LB, Sundquist J, Winkleby M. 2000. Differences in energy, nutrient, and food intakes in a U.S. sample of Mexican American women and men: Findings from the third National Health and Nutrition Examination Survey, 1988–1994. *American Journal of Epidemiology* 152(6):548–557.

Dorfman L, Wilbur P, Lingas EO, Woodruff K, Wallack L. 2005 *Accelerating Policy on Nutrition: Lessons from Tobacco, Alcohol, Firearms, and Traffic Safety.* Final report from a series of meetings conducted by the Berkeley Media Studies Group. Oakland, CA: Public Health Institute.

Duke J, Huhman M, Heitzler C. 2003. Physical activity levels among children aged 9–13 years—United States 2002. *Morbidity and Mortality Weekly Report* 52(33):785–788.

Endicott RC, Brown K, MacDonald S, Schumann M, Ryan M, Sierra J, Wentz L. 2005. *Hispanic Pact Pack. Advertising Age* (Supplement). Pp. 1–51. [Online]. Available: http://www.adage.com/images/random/hispfactpack05.pdf.

Fernandez JR, Redden DT, Pietrobelli A, Allison DB. 2004. Waist circumference percentiles in nationally representative samples of African American, European American, and Mexican American children and adolescents. *Journal of Pediatrics* 145(4):439–444.

Finkelstein EA, Fiebelkorn IC, Wang G. 2004. State-level estimates of annual medical expenditures attributable to obesity. *Obesity Research* 12(1):18–24.

Flores G, Abreu M, Olivar MA, Kastner B. 1998. Access barriers to health care for Latino children. *Archives of Pediatrics and Adolescent Medicine* 152(11):1119–1125.

Food and Nutrition Service. 2005. *Making It Happen! School Nutrition Success Stories.* Alexandria, VA: U.S. Department of Health and Human Services, U.S. Department of Agriculture, and U.S. Department of Education.

Ford ES, Mokdad AH, Ajani UA. 2004. Trends in risk factors for cardiovascular disease among children and adolescents in the United States. *Pediatrics* 114(6):1534–1544.

Freedman DS, Dietz WH, Srinivasan SR, Berenson GS. 1999. The relation of overweight to cardiovascular risk factors among children and adolescents: The Bogalusa Heart Study. *Pediatrics* 103(6):1175–1182.

Freedman DS, Khan LK, Dietz WH, Srinivasan SR, Berenson GS. 2001. Relationship of childhood obesity to coronary heart disease risk factors in adulthood: The Bogalusa Heart Study. *Pediatrics* 108(3):712–718.

Freedman DS, Khan LK, Serdula MK, Galuska DA, Dietz WH. 2002. Trends and correlates of class 3 obesity in the United States from 1990 through 2000. *Journal of the American Medical Association* 288(14):1758–1761.

GAO (U.S. Government Accountability Office). 2005. *Childhood Obesity: Most Experts Identified Physical Activity and the Use of Best Practices as Key to Successful Programs.* GAO-06-127R. Washington, DC: GAO.

Gribble LS, Falciglia G, Davis AM, Couch SC. 2003. A curriculum based on social learning theory emphasizing fruit exposure and positive parent child-feeding strategies: A pilot study. *Journal of the American Dietetic Association* 103(1):100–103.

Hammer L. 2005. Personal communication. Stanford, CA: Medical Director, Center for Health Weight.

Hannon TS, Rao G, Arslanian SA. 2005. Childhood obesity and type 2 diabetes mellitus. *Pediatrics* 116(2):473–480.

Hayden-Wade HA, Stein RI, Ghaderi A, Saelens BE, Zabinski MF, Wilfley DE. 2005. Prevalence, characteristics, and correlates of teasing experiences among overweight children vs. non-overweight peers. *Obesity Research* 13(8):1381–1392.

Heath EM, Coleman KJ. 2002. Evaluation of the institutionalization of the Coordinated Approach to Child Health (CATCH) in a U.S./Mexico border community. *Health Education and Behavior* 29(4):444–460.

Hedley AA, Ogden CL, Johnson CL, Carroll MD, Flegal KM. 2004. Prevalence of overweight and obesity among U.S. children, adolescents, and adults. *Journal of the American Medical Association* 91(23):2847–2850.

Hernandez D. 2004. Children of immigrant families: Demographic changes and the life circumstances of immigrant families. *The Future of Children* 14(2):17–47.

Huhman M, Potter LD, Wong FL, Banspach SW, Duke JC, Heitzler CD. 2005. Effects of a mass media campaign to increase physical activity among children: Year-1 results of the VERB campaign. *Pediatrics* 116(2):e277–e284.

International Life Sciences Institute. 2005. ILSI CHP *Nutrition and Physical Activity Program List.* [Online]. Available: http://chp.ilsi.org/Publications/CHPPhysical ActivityProgramList.htm [accessed April 15, 2006].

IOM (Institute of Medicine). 2005. *Preventing Childhood Obesity: Health in the Balance.* Washington, DC: The National Academies Press.

IOM. 2006. *Food Marketing to Children and Youth: Threat or Opportunity?* Washington, DC: The National Academies Press.

Kahn HS, Imperatore G, Cheng YJ. 2005. A population-based comparison of BMI percentiles and waist-to-height ratio for identifying cardiovascular risk in youth. *Journal of Pediatrics* 146(4):482–488.

Kaplan MS, Huguet N, Newsom JT, McFarland BH. 2004. The association between length of residence and obesity among Hispanic immigrants. *American Journal of Preventive Medicine* 27(4):323–326.

Kaplowitz H, Martorell R, Mendoza F. 1989. Fatness and fat distribution in Mexican American children and youth from the Hispanic Health and Nutrition Examination Survey. *American Journal of Human Biology* 1:631–648.

Katzmarzyk PT, Srinivasan SR, Chen W, Malina RM, Bouchard C, Berenson GS. 2004. Body mass index, waist circumference, and clustering of cardiovascular disease risk factors in a biracial sample of children and adolescents. *Pediatrics* 114:e198–e205.

Kissam E, Intili J, Garcia A. 2003. Spanish-language community radio as a resource for health promotion campaigns targeted to farmworkers and recent immigrants. *Californian Journal of Health Promotion* 1(2):183–197.

Klaudt M, Schetzina K, Mendoza F, Robinson T. 2002. *Racial/Ethnic Differences in Maternal Perception of Children's Weight.* Ambulatory Pediatric Association, Region IX and X, February 2002 Annual Meeting, Carmel, CA.

Kovacs P, Ma L, Hanson RL, Franks P, Stumvoll M, Bogardus C, Baier LJ. 2005. Genetic variation in UCP 2 (uncoupling protein 2) is associated with energy metabolism in Pima Indians. *Diabetologia* 48(11):2292–2295.

Kuczmarski RJ, Ogden CL, Guo SS. 2002. 2000 CDC growth charts for the United States: Methods and development. National Center for Health Statistics. *Vital Health Statistics* 11:246.

Li X, Li S, Ulusoy E, Chen W, Srinivasan SR, Berenson GS. 2004. Childhood adiposity as a predictor of cardiac mass in adulthood: The Bogalusa Heart Study. *Circulation* 110(22):3488–3492.

López R, Barquera S, Hernandez Prado B, Rivera JR. 2006. *Preventing Obesity in Mexican Children and Adolescents.* U.S.–Mexico Workshop on Prevention of Childhood Obesity. Washington, DC: Institute of Medicine.

Malina R, Martorell R, Mendoza F. 1986. Growth status of Mexican American children and youth: Historical trends and contemporary issues. *American Journal of Physical Anthropology* 29(S7):45–79.

Martorell R, Mendoza FS, Castillo RO, Pawson IG, Budge CC. 1987. Short and plump physique of Mexican American children. *American Journal of Physical Anthropology* 73:475–478.

Martorell R, Malina RM, Castillo RO, Mendoza FS, Pawson IG. 1988a. Body proportions in three ethnic groups: Children and youths 2–17 years in NHANES II and HHANES. *Human Biology* 60(2):205–222.

Martorell R, Mendoza F, Castillo R. 1988b. Poverty and stature in children. In: *Linear Growth Retardation in Less Developed Countries.* Waterlow JC. Ed. New York: Raven Press. 14:57–73.

Martorell R, Mendoza F, Castillo R. 1989. Genetic and environmental determinants of growth in Mexican Americans. *Pediatrics* 84(5):864–871.

Maynard MG, Blanck H, Serdula M. 2003. Maternal perception of weight status of children. *Pediatrics* 111:1226–1231.

Mazur RE, Marquis GS, Jensen HH. 2003. Diet and food insufficiency among Hispanic youth: Acculturation and socioeconomic factors in the third National Health and Nutrition Examination Survey. *American Journal of Clinical Nutrition* 78:1120–1127.

Mendoza F, Castillo R. 1986. Growth abnormalities in Mexican-American children in the United States: The NHANES I Study. *Nutrition Research* 6:1247–1257.

Morrison JA, Friedman LA, Harlan WR, Harlan LC, Barton BA, Schreiber GB, Klein DJ. 2005. Development of the metabolic syndrome in black and white adolescent girls: A longitudinal assessment. *Pediatrics* 116(5):1178–1182.

Murphy S, Castillo R, Martorell R, Mendoza F. 1990. An evaluation of the food group intakes by Mexican American children. *Journal of the American Dietetic Association* 90(3):388–393.

Nader MD, Stone EJ, Lytle LA, Perry CL, Osganian SK, Kelder S, Webber LS, Elder JP, Montgomery D, Feldman HA, Wu M, Johnson C, Parcel GS, Luepker RV. 1999. Three-year maintenance of improved diet and physical activity. *Archives of Pediatrics and Adolescent Medicine* 153(7):695–704.

Narayan KM, Boyle JP, Thompson TJ, Sorensen SW, Williamson DF. 2003. Lifetime risk for diabetes mellitus in the United States. *Journal of the American Medical Association* 290(14):1884–1890.

NCHS (National Center for Health Statistics). 2004. *Health, United States, 2004, with Chartbook on Trends in the Health of Americans.* Hyattsville, MD: NCHS.

Neufeld ND, Raffel LJ, Landon C, Chen YD, Vadheim C. 1998. Early presentation of type 2 diabetes in Mexican American youth. *Diabetes Care* 21(1):80–86.

Neuhouser ML, Thompson B, Coronado GD, Solomon CC. 2004. Higher fat intake and lower fruit and vegetables intakes are associated with greater acculturation among Mexicans living in Washington State. *Journal of the American Dietetic Association* 104(1):51–57.

NRC/IOM (National Research Council/Institute of Medicine). 1998. *From Generation to Generation: The Health and Well-Being of Children in Immigrant Families.* Washington, DC: National Academy Press.

NRC/IOM. 1999. *Children of Immigrants: Health, Adjustment, and Public Assistance.* Washington, DC: National Academy Press. Pp. 187–243.

Ogden CL, Flegal KM, Carroll MD, Johnson CL. 2002. Prevalence and trends in overweight among United States children and adolescents, 1999–2000. *Journal of the American Medical Association* 288(14):1728–1732.

Ogden CL, Carroll MD, Curtin LR, McDowell MA, Tabak CJ, Flegal KM. 2006. Prevalence of overweight and obesity in the United States, 1999–2004. *Journal of the American Medical Association* 288295(13):1549–1555.

Olaiz G, Rojas R, Barquera S, Shamah T, Aguilar C, Cravioto P, López P, Hernández M, Tapia R, Sepúlveda J. 2003. *Encuesta Nacional de Salud 2000. Tomo 2. La salud de los adultos.* Cuernavaca, Morelos, México: Instituto Nacional de Salud Pública.

Pelayo R. 2005. Personal communication. Palo Alto, CA: Stanford Sleep Center.

Pietrobelli A, Faith MS, Allison DB, Gallagher D, Chiumello G, Heymsfield SB. 1998. Body mass index as a measure of adiposity among children and adolescents: A validation study. *Journal of Pediatrics* 132(2):204–210.

Pinhas-Hamiel O, Dolan LM, Daniels SR, Standiford D, Khoury PR, Zeitler P. 1996. Increased incidence of non-insulin dependent diabetes mellitus among adolescents. *Journal of Pediatrics* 128:608–615.

Popkin B, Udry JR. 1998. Adolescent obesity increases significantly in second and third generation U.S. immigrants: The national longitudinal study of adolescent health. *Journal of Nutrition* 128:701–706.

Reaven P, Nader PR, Berry C, Hoy T. 1998. Cardiovascular disease insulin risk in Mexican-American and Anglo-American children and mothers. *Pediatrics* 101(4):1–7.

Rivera J, Shamah Levy T, Villalpando Hernández S, González de Cossío T, Hernández Prado B, Sepúlveda J. 2001. *Encuesta Nacional de Nutrición 1999. Estado nutricio de niños y mujeres en México.* Cuernavaca, Morelos, México: Instituto Nacional de Salud Pública.

Rivera JA, Barquera S, Campirano F, Campos I, Safdie M, Tovar V. 2002. Epidemiological and nutritional transition in Mexico: Rapid increase of non-communicable chronic diseases and obesity. *Public Health Nutrition* 5(1A):113–122.

Roberts DF, Foehr UG, Rideout V. 2005. *Generation M: Media in the Lives of 8–18 Year Olds.* KFF. [Online]. Available: http://www.kff.org/entmedia/upload/Generation-M-Media-in-the-Lives-of-8-18-Year-olds-Report.pdf [accessed April 15, 2006].

Romero A, Robinson T, Haydel K, Mendoza F, Killen J. 2004. Association among familism, language preference, and education in Mexican American mothers and their children. *Journal of Developmental and Behavioral Pediatrics* 25(1):34–40.

Ryan AS, Roche AF, Kuczmarski RJ. 1999. Weight, stature, and body mass index data for Mexican Americans from the third national health and nutrition examination survey. *American Journal of Human Biology* 11:673–686.

Salsberry PJ, Reagan PB. 2005. Dynamics of early childhood overweight. *Pediatrics* 116(6):1329.

Sanchez-Castillo CP, Lara JJ, Villa AR, Aguirre J, Escobar M, Gutierrez H, Chavez A, James WP. 2005. Unusually high prevalence rates of obesity in four Mexican rural communities. *Public Health Nutrition* 8(1):53–60.

Schwimmer JB, Burwinkle TM, Varni J. 2003. Health-related quality of life of severely obese children and adolescents. *Journal of the American Medical Association* 289(14):1813–1819.

Shaping America's Youth. 2004. *Shaping America's Youth.* [Online]. Available: http://www. shapingamericasyouth.org/Programs.aspx?page=search [accessed April 15, 2006].

Siegel JM, Yancey AK, Aneshensel CS, Schuler R. 1999. Body image, perceived pubertal timing and adolescent mental health. *Journal of Adolescent Health* 25(2):155–165.

Spooner T, Rainie L. 2001. *Hispanics and the Internet. Pew Internet and American Life Project.* [Online]. Available: http://www.pewinternet.org/PPF/r/38/report_display. asp [accessed April 15, 2006].

Srinivasan SR, Myers L, Berenson GS. 2002. Predictability of childhood adiposity and insulin for developing Insulin Resistance Syndrome (Syndrome X) in young adulthood: The Bogalusa Heart Study. *Diabetes* 51:204–209.

Strauss RS, Pollack HA. 2001. Epidemic increase in childhood overweight, 1986–1998. *Journal of the American Medical Association* 286(22):2845.

Strohl KP, Redline S. 1996. Recognition of obstructive sleep apnea. *American Journal of Respiratory and Critical Care Medicine* 154:279–289.

Thorpe KE, Florence CS, Howard DH, Joski P. 2004. The impact of obesity on rising medical spending. *Health Affairs*. Web Exclusive. October 20:W4-480 to W4-486.

Trevino RP, Hernandez A, Hale DE, Garcia OA, Mobley C. 2005. Impact of the Bienestar school-based diabetes mellitus prevention program on fasting capillary glucose levels: A randomized controlled trial. *Archives of Pediatrics and Adolescent Medicine* 158(9): 911–917.

Trevino RP, Pugh JA, Hernandez AE, Menchaca VD, Ramirez RR, Mendoza M. 1998. Bienestar: A diabetes risk-factor prevention program. *Journal of School Health* 68(2): 62–67.

USPSTF (U.S. Preventive Service Task Force). 2002. *Physical Activity Counseling*. [Online]. Available: http://www.ahrq.gov/clinic/uspstf/uspsphys.htm [accessed April 15, 2006].

USPSTF. 2003. *Healthy Diet Counseling*. [Online]. Available: http://www.ahrq.gov/clinic/uspstf/uspsdiet.htm [accessed April 15, 2006].

Velez-Subervi F. 1999. Spanish-language television coverage of health news. *Howard Journal of Communications* 10(3):207–228.

Wang G, Dietz WH. 2002. Economic burden of obesity in youths aged 6–17 years. *Pediatrics* 109(5):e81–e87.

Whitaker RC. 2004. Predicting preschooler obesity at birth: The role of maternal obesity in early pregnancy. *Pediatrics* 114(1):e29.

Whitlock EP, Williams SB, Gold R, Smith PR, Shipman SA. 2005. Screening and interventions for childhood overweight: A summary of evidence for the U.S. Preventive Services Task Force. *Pediatrics* 116(1):e125–e144.

Williams DE, Cadwell BL, Cheng YJ, Cowie CC, Gregg EW, Geiss LS, Engelgau MM, Narayan KM, Imperatore G. 2005. Prevalence of impaired fasting glucose and its relationship with cardiovascular disease risk factors in U.S. adolescents, 1999–2000. *Pediatrics* 116(5):1122–1126.

Yusuf S, Hawken S, Ounpuu S, Bautista L, Franzosi MG, Commerford P, Lang CC, Rumboldt Z, Onen CL, Lisheng L, Tanomsup S, Wangai P Jr, Razak F, Sharma AM, Anand SS, INTERHEART Study Investigators. 2005. Obesity and the risk of myocardial infarction in 27,000 participants from 52 countries: A case-control study. *Lancet* 366(9497):1640–1649.

PART II
POSTRES

The Art of Cooking

Encarnación Pinedo

This is one of the arts that very few of those who are called chefs possess in perfection: and even though it is considered one of the most essential accomplishments, its study seems to have been ignored among families in these modern times. In earlier times, the people of the Middle Ages had more or less mastered it, always in accordance with the wealth, opulence, potential, and social position of each nation and its people.

The Persians, said Herodotus, had the custom of celebrating their birthdays, and it was only then that they had great feasts and sacrificed one of their most valued domestic animals to their gods: they roasted it in a barbecue with the finest spices, and all their people dined.

The Greeks were fine gourmets, even though the foods and soups of the Athenians were ridiculed for their frugality.

Notwithstanding that Athenaeus, Archestratus, and many others wrote books about cooking, those all came to be meaningless, because each tribe had the custom of eating different foods. Fish was the only flesh that was commonly used.

To give an idea of the extravagant manner in which they proclaimed their recipes, Archestratus spoke of a "ray cooked in oil, wine and aromatic herbs, with a little grated cheese. Fish stuffed with little fish balls and fried; cooked in marinade; roasted in fig leaves; refreshed in oil; roasted in ashes"; and so on. Such are the recipes they gave.

The Egyptians had the reputation of being great bread eaters, and although they had the finest flours, they made their dough solely with the fruit of a tree called "lotus" or of spelt, a species of wheat that was dried and beaten.[1]

Fish were salted and dried in the sun. Partridges, ducks, and all kinds of small birds were salted and eaten raw. On the occasion of a festival or other rare event, they assuredly ate roasted or cooked beef.

The Romans had their barley gruels called "pulses," and these were the principal food of the people, together with all kinds of vegetables. Very little meat was used. Lucullus introduced some new ideas in the art of cooking,

Encarnación Pinedo, "The Art of Cooking," included in *Encarnación's Kitchen: Mexican Recipes from Nineteenth-Century California*. Edited and translated by Dan Strehl. With an essay by Victor Valle. Berkeley: University of California Press, 2003. Used by permission.

and Apicius earned a reputation that made him celebrated in this art as it then existed. The Romans almost always prepared and cooked their foods with oil.

The Germans seem to have given little or no importance to the style in which their meals were prepared.

The English have advanced the art a bit, enough that several of its writers have published on the subject: a Mr. Pegge in 1390, Sir J. Elliot in 1539, Abraham Veale in 1575, and Widovas Treasure in 1625. Despite all this, there is not a single Englishman who can cook, as their foods and style of seasoning are the most insipid and tasteless that one can imagine.

The French and Italians have been the most advanced, although the French system was very imperfect until the Italian taste was introduced in France by the princesses of the royal house of the Medici; since then the excellence of the French makes them the best cooks in the world. They discovered that meats could and ought to be basted with their own juices or broths while they were cooking.

The esteem of a good chef can only be known when we take note of the wages they earn in the opulent homes of affluent families, in first-class hotels, and in clubs of prominent persons in large and populous cities.

The truth is that in our times it is thought that this art is one of the most enviable accomplishments of a woman; and it is now treated as one of the most precious and necessary branches of her education, so much so that in England and in the United States today, schools of cooking have been established, even though without a very happy result; it seems generally that only young women of a humble and poor lineage dedicate themselves to this very important study.

I am quite convinced that the time has come when the knowledge of cooking will be obligatory; and the art will receive a major impetus because the great importance of knowing how to prepare, season, and temper foods for the fire, making them ready to help in the digestion in the human stomach, will become evident; and I have resolved to publish this book, which I have entitled *The Spanish Cook without Equal*, because its like has never been brought to light, so explicit, complete, and compendious, with long explanations and details for cooking in all styles and with the greatest ease.

For the benefit of my subscribers I offer the following advice, which I hope will not seem excessive, when one takes into account that ninety-nine out of one hundred cooks don't know what I am speaking about, but they should know the following.

KITCHEN CLEANLINESS

Cleanliness is undoubtedly the cardinal virtue of every cook.

Foods are much more appetizing and healthy when they are cooked in a clean and tidy manner.

Many lives have been sacrificed because of a lack of cleanliness in bronze, copper, and ceramic pots; the first two types must always be kept lustrous and clean inside and out; they can and should be cleaned on the inside with salt and hot vinegar every time you want to cook something in them, and no greasy or acid substance should be allowed to set in them after it has been cooked.

Everything in the kitchen should be maintained with the greatest cleanliness possible, and leftovers or scraps and the rest of food not used for the preparation of soups should be thrown out the moment it is no longer needed.

The same observations that were made with respect to copper kitchenware and so on are applicable to all utensils and the clothing of a good cook, who should have these fundamental objectives: first, cook all your dishes and soups according to the requirements of the rules of the art; and secondly, be pure and clean, in your person and in your work, for that way you will always merit the praises of your patrons or admirers: then, as we said before, *cleanliness is the cardinal virtue of the cook.*

And now, since cooks need to use some judgment in their work, I do not think it is unreasonable for me to give some advice here, consistent with my extensive experience and study of this enviable art.

We start with the principle that all who sit down at table to eat expect good food; and we cannot pardon mistakes made by the cook, or give excuses when the palate ends up unhappy after having paid good money.

When meat forms the principal part of the meal, one must know if it is of good or bad quality, and this is how:

When the meat from a steer is good, it should be relaxed and red, and the fat yellowish. The meat from a cow, on the contrary, should have a fine grain and be more faded, and the fat should be medium white. Bad meat is obtained from animals badly fed or too old; it can be spotted in the hardness of the fat, blackish and corroded meat, and in the thick nerves across the ribs. When you press a piece of meat and it springs back after you remove your fingers, you can be sure that the animal is good and healthy and in its prime. When you press a piece of meat with your finger, if it does not rise promptly after removing the finger, nor recover the imprint made by the pressure, the animal was old and maybe ill, or at least of an inferior quality, and you should not use the meat.

The meat from beef is cooked or roasted in the styles indicated by the recipes in this book.

SELECTING INGREDIENTS

The Jewish prohibition against the meat of pork, as a dirty food, was based on the intrinsic uncleanness of this animal.

An article appeared in one of the monthly magazines that gave a succinct report of the sickly constitution of the pig. The article said that in Vermont, New Hampshire, Maine, and other eastern states, where the inhabitants must vaccinate their livestock, almost all the pigs sent to the market in Boston, and there are thousands of them, are sick with scrofula, salt phlegm, rashes, herpes, and bad blood humors. These and many other calamities can occur through the use of meat from sick pigs, and the famous Dr. Brainard assured the author that it has been calculated, and with reason, that more than half the pigs in this country are unhealthy. You must use good judgment and care to select a suckling pig or a piece of pork to cook.

The cook should be convinced that the pork was fattened only with grain or clean food, or that the mothers of the suckling pigs were from the farm and were fattened purely with corn and other clean and nutritious grain.

The ways to make stews with pork are listed in their appropriate place.

The same rules given above for selecting beef serve for lamb.

To select poultry, watch for the following: if a cock, there should be small, unclipped spurs, and if a hen, it should have smooth crest and feet. When you buy dead ones be careful to smell them carefully, and feel the breast to see if they have meat there. If not, it is probable that they died from illness and shouldn't be eaten.

The way to choose a goose is as follows: If the goose is young, it should have a yellow beak; a red beak is a sign of age. If it is fresh, it should have very flexible feet when dead; if they are rigid, the bird is old and dry.

In selecting fish, of whatever species, only look to see if the eyes are brilliant and the body rigid and very straight; this is an infallible sign that it is fresh.

Select eggs by putting them in a pan of water, if they stay on the bottom, they are good; if they stand on their points, they are bad and should not be eaten.

You can tell when flour is good by taking a fistful in your hand and squeezing it firmly: if it compacts and stays in a mass, it is of the best quality, and the dough you make from it will be smooth, flexible, and elastic. An adulterated flour is much heavier than the better flour, and is hard to compress; if you try it as described above, it will not give the same result.

Second—take a small quantity and rub between your fingers; if it is smooth and flexible, it is good, and if it is sticky and rough, it is bad.

Third—put a little bit on the table and blow softly with your breath; if it leaves little piles on the table that resisted the action of the breath, it is good, and if it completely spreads out, it is bad.

Fourth—put a thimbleful in the palm of your hand and rub smoothly with your finger: if the flour smooths out and stays slippery, it is of an inferior quality; and if, on the contrary, it seems rough in the hand, like fine sand, it is good.

Mushrooms are one of the most dangerous condiments, and the way of knowing for certain is the following: take the mushroom and put salt in the spongy part underneath; if it turns yellow, it is poisonous, but if it turns black, it is good.

Butter is clarified in a hot bath. Allow it to settle and pour off only the clear part, cooling it as soon as possible. Butter clarified in this way will stay good and fresh a long time.

Rancid butter is fixed this way: boil it in water with a little charcoal (let us say a tenth part) to remove the rancidity. Once it is melted, let it rise to the surface and leave it to settle, then take it out carefully with a spoon. It will remain absolutely fresh, but it will lose the flavor of table butter and can only be used in stews in the kitchen.

Select nutmeg by pricking it with a pin: if oil comes out, it is good.

GENERAL PRINCIPLES

It is preferable to use a small pan or an enamel pot to make preserves or jams and good white sugar, but never beet sugar.

The good cook ought to have a supply of various spices. Some dishes, and the most exquisite ones, cannot be made without them. Whole-grain pepper is preferable to ground.

OBSERVATIONS

First—you should never let jams cool in a copper vessel, because of verdigris.

Second—you should examine the papers that cover them from time to time, and change them if they are damaged.

Third—when preserves show the least thing that would make you throw them out, you can boil them for a few minutes, but they lose their flavor.

Fourth—you must keep preserves in a cool place, but sheltered from humidity. Heat starts a fermentation that progresses quickly, and the humidity makes them moldy.

SOPAS • SOUPS

ALBÓNDIGAS A LA ESPAÑOLA

SPANISH-STYLE MEATBALL SOUP

Chop pork loin until it is minced or ground, and remove any sinews. Then add finely chopped green onion, peeled and seeded tomatoes, parsley, fresh or dry coriander, and garlic.

Add a piece of cornmeal paste [*nixtamal*] or a spoonful of cornmeal, one or two raw eggs, bread crumbs, a piece of lard or butter, salt, and pepper.

Mix these together by hand, forming meatballs as usual, then add them to the boiling stock. If there is no stock, cook in boiling water.

Season the broth with tomato, green onion, chopped parsley, salt, pepper, and butter. Thicken the broth with beaten egg yolks when ready to serve.

MOLE

MOLE DE CARNERO

LAMB MOLE

Toast, devein, and fry equal quantities of ancho and pasilla chiles; then toast the seeds of the same chiles and grind them with peanuts, clove, and cinnamon. Put this on to fry, and break up the chiles in it. Then when it all comes together, add hot water and salt. Take great care that it does not get watery, and then add the cooked meat and let it simmer.

MORCILLA • BLOOD SAUSAGE

MORCILLA NEGRA A LA ESPAÑOLA

SPANISH-STYLE BLACK BLOOD SAUSAGE

Black blood sausage is made with pig's blood.

Take the blood from the pig and put it into a pot. Put in a spoonful of salt. This will set the blood even if it is hot. The blood needs to be beaten and then passed through a sieve before it coagulates.

Peel an onion and cut in small cubes. Get the best lard from the inside of the pig and chop it in very small squares with two ground garlic cloves, finely minced mint, two teaspoons of red-chile seeds, and pepper.

Mix all of this with the blood, and add very fresh, rich milk. For two half liters of blood, add two small cups of milk.

Stir, and when it reaches a good consistency, fill casings that have been properly cleaned and prepared.

Tie both ends of each sausage with a string, making each the size you wish.

Place inside a casserole a few at a time, in very hot water, but not hot enough for them to boil. Carefully turn them from time to time, and add cold water to the casserole so they do not burst. Let them cook until the blood coagulates firmly, which you can tell if no blood drops come out when you prick them.

Remove from the water and hang them to air-dry.

CALABAZAS • SQUASH

CALABACITAS RELLENAS

Stuffed Squash

Hollow out both ends with the end of a scoop or a cooking spoon, stuff them with a *picadillo* or with cheese, cover the opening with pieces of turnip cut in the shape of a cork, place in a pot lined with slices of ham, cover with some broth, and cook over a low fire.

Serve with tomato sauce.

CALABACITAS EN MANTEQUILLA

Squash in Butter

Cut the squash in quarters, and cook in water.

When done, take them out of the water, leaving just a little. Serve them with butter, grated cheese, salt, and pepper.

CALABACITAS A LA MEXICANA

Mexican-Style Squash

Slice the squash and simmer in lightly salted water. Put them in a napkin to drain all the water they contain. Then dip in beaten egg and fry in very hot lard. When done, elegantly make a layer of squash, cover with plenty of grated cheese and butter, and continue to layer, finishing with a layer of cheese.

Make these layers on a platter, which is put in the oven so they can be served very hot.

CEBOLLAS • ONIONS

CEBOLLAS EN LA CAZUELA

ONIONS IN A CASSEROLE

Choose some medium-sized onions and peel them, putting them in the bottom of a casserole with a little butter. Then add a glass of water, salt, pepper, and a little sugar. Cook on a high fire until the sauce has almost disappeared. Then put them in a serving dish; splash with a few drops of vinegar, a little chopped parsley, and the water from the casserole. Let the sauce simmer, and pour it over the onions, which should be served hot.

CHICHAROS VERDES A LA ESPAÑOLA

SPANISH-STYLE GREEN PEAS

Put a good piece of lard in a casserole and, when good and hot, add a finely chopped green onion, one or two tablespoons of tomato, salt, pepper, and a tablespoon of sugar.

Let the tomato simmer for a few minutes, then add the freshly shelled peas.

Sauté over a low fire, stirring so they do not stick to the bottom of the pan. Add a little water, cover the pot, and let it cook for a while on low heat.

SALSAS • SAUCES

SALSA, O EL ADORNO DE UNA MESA

SAUCE, OR THE ORNAMENT OF THE TABLE

Cut two pounds of beef in the shape of fat fingers, another [pound] of ham, two large carrots, and three onions.

Put it all in a large casserole over the fire, and add a pound of butter, the juice of three or four lemons, three cloves, a little basil, two chopped bay leaves, a little thyme, pepper, and the corresponding salt. Simmer until it has reduced by half; take it off the fire, and pour in a ceramic jar to use when you need.

JARABE • SYRUP

JARABE DE ZUMO DE LIMÓN

LEMON SYRUP

Make a clear syrup with three pounds of sugar, and when it starts to thicken, add a quart of juice from very ripe lemons.

Let it finish boiling, take it off the heat, let it cool, and put [it] in bottles.

JARABE DE MORA

BLACKBERRY SYRUP

Squeeze some very black blackberries, slightly before they are perfectly ripe, and put twenty-four ounces of juice in thick syrup, made with a pound of sugar. Let it all boil together for a few minutes: take it off the fire, let cool, and put [it] in dry bottles covered well.

Advice: to know if the syrup is ready, let a drop fall on a plate; if the liquid that falls scatters into many drops, you need to cook it longer, until the drop that you pour on the plate does not scatter. This is the test for knowing when you have reached the right point.

JARABE O CREMA DE FRAMBUESAS

RASPBERRY SYRUP OR CREAM

To two quarts of good brandy add half a quart of raspberry syrup made like blackberry syrup.

JARABE DE HORCHATA A LA ESPAÑOLA

SPANISH-STYLE ALMOND SYRUP

Take a pound of sweet almonds, two pounds of sugar, four ounces of bitter almonds, a half gallon of water, two ounces of orange-blossom water, and the rind of a lemon.

Leave the almonds in cold water long enough so that they can be easily peeled; don't use hot water as you usually do. Crush the almonds in a mortar, from time to time adding a little water and the lemon rind.

Make a paste, and dissolve with half the water, squeezing it strongly through a thick napkin, return the paste to the mortar, add water, and squeeze it again.

After this, bring some water in a pan to a boil and pour in the almond milk, stirring it until it has boiled for a few minutes.

Next, remove it from the fire and let it cool, add the orange-blossom water, and pass everything through a napkin.

Fill the bottles with this syrup, checking them from time to time, because the almond oil floats, since it is very light, and tends to separate into two parts, and the syrup can change if you do not take the precaution of shaking it to keep the syrup properly emulsified.

NOTES

1. Although described this way by classical authors Theophrastus, Diodorus, and Pliny, "lotus tree" bread was actually made from the aquatic lotus. Spelt was never found in ancient Egypt, and the wheat she refers to was in fact emmer (William J. Darby, *Food: The Gift of Osiris* [New York: Academic Press, 1977], vol. 2, pp. 489, 522, 642).—*Translator*

Los Paleteros

Camilo José Vergara

The ice-cream trucks of Los Angeles are too slow for the freeways. Built at least a quarter of a century ago and constantly in need of repair, each vehicle is unique. These trucks are painted vibrant colors that appeal to children, and the roofs are raised up so that the driver can walk around and work inside. Awkwardly tall and narrow, these ornately decorated trucks, known as *trocas*, are moving works of folk art. Their drivers are known as *paleteros*, a name derived from the *paletas* (wooden sticks) inside the ice-cream bars.

I have visited the special ice-cream truck parking lots. The drivers are mostly young Mexican men. A few married couples work together, and some bring their children along as helpers. One told me, "Behind each of these little trocas, there is a life, a family." A small business on wheels, the occupation has not changed much since the time of horse-drawn carriages. In Mexico, paleteros use pushcarts to do business, but recently, a few ice-cream trucks have been introduced by returning drivers who have learned the trade in the United States.

The paleteros often don't know the titles of the melodies they play endlessly as they cruise along. Knowing that Disney tunes are popular with their young clientele, however, one paletero may buy a cassette at a thrift store and share it with his fellows to copy. "If the trocas played Mexican *rancheras*, the children would not come out to buy; it is not the music they expect," said Luis. That explains why all the trucks play similar tunes.

Working in the most dangerous areas of L.A., paleteros often confront armed robbers and vandals. A woman driver summed up the life on the road to me: "One gets stoned, shot, and run over. Paleteros suffer very much." Her words sounded like the lyrics of a Mexican *corrido*. A driver who was listening in added, "People get inside the truck to steal the money and the merchandise."

In one parking lot alone, accommodating seventy trucks, three drivers have been killed during the past six years. A former driver named Marco

Camilo José Vergara, "Los Paleteros," published in *La Vida Latina en L.A./Urban Latino Cultures*, edited by Gustavo Leclerc, Raul Villa, and Michael J. Daer. Thousand Oaks: Sage Publications, Publisher in association with the Southern California Studies Center of the University of Southern California, 1999. Used by permission.

Antonio recalled the panic he experienced when he stopped for a light and a man put a gun to his head and demanded his wallet. Soon after, he quit driving and took a job as a janitor in a hospital. Paleteros fear not only for themselves but also for their customers, especially the small children who might get run over.

To defend themselves, the owners transform their vehicles into fortresses. Selling takes place through a small window barely big enough for a can of soda. The truck exteriors display Disney characters, reinforced doors, and iron grates. José explained that he had to work behind bars because otherwise someone could pull him by the hair and steal his things.

Paleteros try to keep their vehicles free of graffiti. A driver told me that when the truck stops, five or six teenagers often surround it and spray paint it. "What can you do?" he asks. To keep his truck from being defaced, Mario painted a large image of the Virgin of Guadalupe on its side, flanked by the flags of Mexico and the United States. Proud of his art, he tells me that the Virgin keeps his troca free of graffiti and protects him on his rounds.

A paletero makes between $30 and $60 a day, about as much as working in a sweatshop: But he is his own boss and spends time out in the open. This business requires little capital to get started, and the driver, according to the manager of a parking lot, "does not need to worry about a work permit." They need only pass inspection from the health department and obtain a $250 license.

A used truck costs from $1,500 to $2,500 plus the month's parking, the electricity needed to keep the refrigerator running, and the services of a night watchman—in all, an extra $50. Homeowners park their vehicles in their backyards, but most paleteros are renters, and their landlords won't let them connect the trucks to their houses.

A few paleteros supplement their earnings selling nachos, hot dogs, even produce, without a food license, thus risking fines of $100 or more. Others own more than one truck and rent them to others. Having a second job as a janitor, factory worker, or parking lot attendant is common. A few owners—tired of the dangers and meager rewards of the job—transform their vehicles into moving vans or use them for storage. There are even those who gut the interiors and rent the trucks out as a cheap place to live. Some are able to save enough to start their own businesses. One paletero from South Central, now a baker, has parked his truck in his backyard, where it waits. If he fails as a baker, he can return to being a paletero without going through unemployment.

Despite working in such a dangerous and badly rewarded occupation, many paleteros seemed cheerful. Silda, a former paletera agreed with me, commenting,

> They don't have anybody to give them orders, they don't have a boss. Nobody can tell them that they have to work tomorrow. Nobody tells them when it's time to quit. One suffers a lot during the cold and rainy season, from December to January. Then one does not even make enough to pay the rent. But during the hot days, one makes good money.

Luis, the manager of a parking lot, felt that paleteros were very happy with the freedom they have in their job and that they laughed and joked in the secure environment of the parking lot. Once in the streets, "They are worried. Sometimes, they are robbed as they start the day and have no money with them."

Tomato Potatoe, Chalupa Shaloopa

Dagoberto Gilb

Let me describe plate #3 at every local Authenic Mexican Restaurant 50 years ago. Imagine an oval, particularly thick ceramic plate being hustled over straight out of an oven, so hot it can only be delivered with a potholder and a warning to never ever touch—it's a hot, hot plate each recipient, individually, will be uniquely told—that is set down a distance from the edge of the table so it won't burn chest hairs, or whatever, and the clothes in between. The re-fried beans are gurgling and the "Spanish" rice is reconstituting into its dry grain state, the peas and carrot chunks mutating away from the vegetable cat-egory, and the red sauce of the enchiladas is bubbling, the yellow and white cheese topping still sizzling from being on the verge of burning. Wait long enough so the plate can be handled. Then, go on, tip it sideways. Tip it upside down. Toss it to practice dexterity, letting it roll over and over, and catch it. Spin it on a finger like a top, food side down, or roll it on its edge across a long banquet table. Yes, the tablespoon of shredded iceberg lettuce and that thin, very thin slice of a too-green red tomato—colorful garnish—that nobody ever eats anyway, both of them wilted and dehydrated, will fall off. But the rest? Nope. It's a Mexican Frisbee!

The Mexican plate #3 was—and of course still is, more often than not—what Americans were served at Mexican restaurants miles north of the entire stretch of the border: tortillas or masa fried or soaked into lots of heavy oil or kneaded in lard, the least expensive ground chuck beef, fatty colored cheese packaged in huge, discount blocks. It is this food that Glen Bell, World War II Marine Corps veteran and owner of Bell's Drive-In hot dog stand ate and loved and riffed on until, in San Bernardino, Redlands, and Riverside, a des-ert agricultural region of Southern California, he established the first three fast-food taco stands featuring Mexican food, Taco Tia, which eventually was transformed into the mega-chain all America knows for its ad slogans "Run for the Border" and "*Yo quiero* Taco Bell" and its Chihuahua dog, not to mention those famed crackly tacos.

Dagoberto Gilb, "Tomato Potatoe, Chalupa Shaloopa" from *Lengua Fresca: Latinos Writing on the Edge*, edited by Harold Augenbraum and Ilan Stavans, Mariner Books, 2006, pp. 81–90. Used by permission.

I remember when I first encountered what might be called hippie "fusion" Mexican food. I was in Isla Vista, California, a university community where a Bank of America was burned in a student riot that brought out the National Guard in 1970, an era and community where Mr. Kinko opened his first copy shop and that incubated the health and organic food rebellion, believing both would lead to the political contrary of what are now corporate enterprises. For someone like me who'd been raised in the big city, near rainbow-streaked, inky pools left from leaking oil pans, distracted by moonlit twinkles of broken half-pints and beer bottles smashed against a curb, the only green growth I really thought about was always in someone else's wallet. In Isla Vista, I saw lettuce and kale and collard grow in public hippie gardens. I was taught how to cut off fresh broccoli, and I learned to cook it too. I even got used to cauliflower if it had a good cheese sauce on it. But I sincerely thought things were going way too wacky when I went to an Isla Vista Mexican restaurant that had the bizarre cultural audacity to put alfalfa sprouts in a burrito. I grew up, for example, loving Chinese food, though not really those bean sprouts, but I didn't complain when I ate them—you just put enough soy and hot sauce over it all. But alfalfa sprouts in a burrito? *N'hombre, que pinche desmadre!*

Until I started liking it. And then I began to like the idea of it. I liked, for example, the idea of frijoles without that yummy bacon fat that was saved in the coffee can by the sink, or refried days and days after in a scoop or so of Crisco. I was changing with the times too, sure, but I had always loved fresh cooked mushrooms and corn served in butter or lemon, and avocado raw or mashed, and of course fresh jalapeños and serranos, and there was no store fruit made or invented—oh yeah, *grown*, on trees—that I didn't seek out. Where I came up, if you were a guy who made a point of eating that decorative slice of tomato—you know, intentionally and not by accident—there were dudes around that would ask you how hot pink your panties were. I was the kind of tough who'd shake his head at one of those *panzones*, especially if he wasn't too much bigger than me, and reach over and take the slice off his plate too.

Plate #3 is not the national plate of Mexico. Mexican food is diverse, if not one of the most complicated cuisines, competitive with Europe's. Even enchiladas aren't really a lasagna of cheese and *carne picada* and chopped onion wrapped in an oil-sogged tortilla; at its purest an enchilada is, first, dredged in chile (hence, "in chile" equals *enchilada*), then filled with what amounts to a taste of meat or cheese, which then, traditionally, gets a sprinkle of crumbly white fresh cheese, or *queso fresco*. Enchiladas and tacos are most often not primary meals. Fish is plentiful because there are ocean coasts on either side of the country. And vegetables, including *nopales*, and peppers, and squash. One of my favorite tacos was of sweet onions with *rajas de chile* in Matamoros. I love the ceviche both in Ensenada, Baja California, and Echo Park, Los Angeles. I love the huevos rancheros, with extra *chile de arból* over it, at Lucy's in El Paso. My favorite Mexican restaurant in Austin offers tacos *de espinaca* and *hongo*, and I'm sorry, that's not hippie, that's Mexican. I have eaten the best *pozole* ever in Mexico City, and *taquerias* there only cook straight off a grill near the sidewalk, no fried or ovened anything.

Mexican food is not, by nature, unhealthy—or not more so than French or even Chinese food is. Yet Taco Bell romanticizes the most fattening character of both popular American and Mexican food—it cannot be only a historical irony that this business symbiotically evolved out of and alongside the hot dog and hamburger culture (McDonald's Ray Kroc, a friend of Bell's, opened his first hamburger stand in San Bernardino, and Glen Bell's early business partner became the founder of the Del Taco chain, while Bell's wife came up with the ungrammatical German name for another friend's fledgling business, Der Wienerschnitzel). I would even go so far as to claim that plate #3 was and is not the most common meal in Mexican American homes, in the same way that chop suey was and is not in Chinese American homes. Inexpensive dishes are often created and eaten in the hungriest, make-the-best-of-it times, and poor people eat poor meals with poor products. But I'd even go a step further. That the #3—well, maybe #5, with two beef tacos as well, the corn tortillas and the meat inside deep-fried—is what Anglos, not Mexicans, identified as Mexican food because the Mexican restaurants catered to them and their dinner money, as one in San Bernardino did to Mr. Bell.

But consider what has happened in the most populated Mexican American cities at and near the Texas border—El Paso and San Antonio. El Paso in particular is overwhelmed by fast-food and national chain restaurants and virtually nothing else. Even Chico's Tacos is a city institution most adored for its cheap hot dogs, burgers, and french fries, while the Hamburger Inn is known for the best of Sunday *menudo*—fresh oregano and dried chile and chopped onion and limes—on any late night. It might be that San Antonio has an equal number of chain food joints, but what has to be like three fourths of the central city's restaurants are making tacos, and it seems like the competition is as much about who's the closest to 99¢. Breakfast tacos are always of egg and chorizo or potato or *papas con chorizo* or wienie or ham or country sausage or *machacado*. Lunch tacos can be *carne guisada*, *picadillo, chicharron,* country sausage, beef or chicken fajita, *carnitas, lengua, carne asada*—OK, one of guacamole, another of beans, but aside from that, and a spoonful of *tomate* blended for the *salsa de chile*, not a vegetable in the place, and there are no fruits for dessert. These are not tacos made with deep-fried corn tortillas. They are handmade on the spot and toasted on a grill and they are flour. They are good. The fluffiness of flour tortillas comes from the *manteca*. The fluffier they are, the more lard.

OK, though I do love healthy food, like everyone, I also love fluffy flour tortillas, the same as everyone does chocolate cake. I happen to love lightly fried corn tortillas—sprinkle salt on it while it's still hot, even a little *limón*, and I don't even need a filling. I love french fries fried with chorizo. I love too much cheese. There isn't a taco listed above I don't love to eat. I love fast-food burgers, especially if I can layer them with some slices of fresh or marinated jalapeño. I love Polish hot dogs. *Hijole,* I love fried bologna sandwiches with Tapatío hot sauce! I love tamales, green, red, or sweet. But. But, except, the problem is: it's the fluffiness portion again, and "the best" tamales are like 50 percent *manteca* fluffy!

While the filming proceeded on the latest version of *The Alamo* a couple of years ago, the gossip around the Austin movie scene was that there was trouble casting a Mexican army, which, in that other century, was especially hungry—which is to say, not so fat. I have not checked to see if the gossip was true, but you don't have to be looking for extras to notice. For example, I was in the sweetest hidden-away taco restaurant in San Antonio on a recent Sunday. Decorative tinsel frills of blue, silver, green, gold, and red crisscrossed the ceiling, the walls were lime green, the plastic tablecloths were blue-white, the dark carpet had lavender flowers, the chairs were orange vinyl, and there were probably seventy-five of them, and you had to wait for a table for *lonche*. The only thin person there was a woman maybe ninety years old with a walker. How many breakfast tacos can possibly fit between a tight belt and the memory of a small waist? How many flour tortillas? Let's not play around with it—just look at the schoolyards! Of course the explanation is not that there's such an overabundance of wealth we feast at a gluttonous Henry VIII banquet table. Some like to defend the bulk, calling it all a genetic propensity. Probably it is, especially while even that thin slice of tomato is avoided. It's that *lo barato sale caro*. That is, it's poverty, the food of the undereducated and underpaid, unexposed and untraveled ones who find *tacos de espinaca y hongo* weird and who find, in a taco of *huevos con wienie* and a Texas-sized Coke, the satisfying comfort of home.

Though it's really meant to be a drive-through experience, I recently spent an hour, 6–7 P.M., with a *muy* sugary sweet lemonade inside a South Austin Taco Bell. I will say, no offense, it brings on a strange motel-like experience. The music: Elton John, Natalie Merchant, Carly Simon, Bob Seeger. The patrons: a fat, graying, kind-looking white guy with a baseball cap and a mentally disabled Mexican American he clearly took care of, who was probably the same age, give or take. A very fat black couple. A way fat Mexican American guy alone. A Mexican American mom, a little heavy, and her cute overweight daughter, who went to refill her oil-drum-sized soda cup before they left. A family walked in, or what seemed like one, Mexican American, a mom and her three big teenage sons. Only one of the boys was a lot of belly soft; the others might just be called big kids. They were laughing, happy, which resonated in the punishing stillness that had been there. Just because that Taco Bell advertising push was driving me insane, as the cashier who sold me my drink, a scrawny white teenager with black-rimmed glasses, came near to pull out the full trash bag and replace it with a new plastic liner, I asked him to tell me what a chalupa was. You see, BTB—that is, Before Taco Bell—I thought I knew what a chalupa looked like, but then I am dumb. He described the meat and the cheese and lettuce and that it was inside a fried shell. I mean, I asked, how's it different from a taco? It's bigger, he said. That *is* exactly how it seems in its beautiful photo-shoot poses: just like a taco, which beside the big chalupa looks like a little boy, while his daddy is a hefty, NFL pro, grown up. So, I asked, how's the shell different from the taco's shell? It's thicker, he answered.

This South Austin Taco Bell is in a compact neighborhood of very rich, rich, middle, lower-middle, poor, and homeless. All the racial cross-section and mix is seen here. Sharing the same asphalted area are, on its east, an old-school McDonald's, and on its west a Goodyear Tire and Car Care Center. Across the street are, among others, a Radio Shack and a Dollar Store and a popular Family Thrift Store, a Rosie's Tamale House (not so great) and a Mandarin Chinese place (kind of too sticky and spooky dark inside to even trust the takeout). It's not more than a couple of blocks away from good Mexican restaurants. La Nueva Onda specializes in breakfast tacos and *fideo* bowls. Curra's serves the best from the interior of Mexico, like *pibil* and *mixiote*, maintaining the finest tequilas, and it's not that far west to Polvo's, where lots of vegetables come with most *platos*, or from the meat market Moreliana's, where tacos here are like tacos across and the *chile de aguacate* makes both Mexicans and non-Mexicans want to celebrate with a *grito*.

What I'm saying is that when I went into the Taco Bell the next time, for lunch, it was willful. I couldn't remember what one of those tacos tasted like. Like everyone else, I had relented, to be polite to others, once or twice in my teenage years. So long ago, it seemed like BTB. And here's the truth—I was afraid I would outright like the taco. I mean, I know I shouldn't, but, bad, I sneak a Mega Grab Doritos now and then and I eat too many tortilla chips at Polvo's before I get my favorite fish dinner and I used to really like cheap hamburgers and so how could I not think, if unhealthy like the aforementioned, I wouldn't like a taco that would be a combo of all those with some curls of cheese and ribbons of iceberg lettuce and a few tomato chunks that were now a settled source of a union dispute? I arrived at the same time as a cute, thin Chicana did—I opened the door for her and she ordered first. She was eating there. I'd say, by her voice, she didn't know Spanish. At my turn I ask this cashier, just to hear his answer, what a chalupa is. This cashier I swear is the same black dude at the corner up the street at the highway on-ramp who up and back walks a cardboard sign, "Anything Will Help." He turns and points to the image of a big chalupa on the framed plastic menu. What's in it? I ask. When he starts to read to me, very slowly, the description off the menu, I stop him. I order one chalupa and one taco, to go, and I wait, listening to Norah Jones. At the drive-up window, the young woman with the headset is talking English comfortably into the mike but switches into a more comfortable Spanish with another woman employee I can't see, who speaks Spanish so strong I'd bet she probably struggles with English. A black woman announces my number, knowing it's mine before I can find first the receipt and then the number on it, winking, and I grab a handful of the "fire" packets of hot sauce and throw them into the "Spice Up the Night" bag and set myself up once I get home.

How's a Taco Bell chalupa not like a Taco Bell taco? It is a lot bigger, maybe by two. The beef one I bought had sour cream in it. But the shell, well, it is not corn like the taco's but is a thick white flour pita bread that has been fried on the outside so that it keeps its *U* shape but isn't hard inside. The main filling in both was the meat, the beef, what would be *picadillo* on a Mexican food menu. I ate them both, and let me tell you unvaguely, directly reflecting the complete and utter surprise that I myself did not anticipate, how genuinely awful the meat was. Spiced, if you'll excuse the expression, somewhere between very lousy chili and the worst jar of spaghetti meat sauce, only a lot less good, it was so bad it doesn't even matter for me to say I didn't like the taste of that chalupa shell much or that the taco's shell wasn't nearly as good as the cheapest generic grocery store tortilla chips, because those are complaints along the lines of griping that Wal-Mart doesn't have a fine enough selection of clothing. I won't even bother to be polite and say that I liked the sour cream, you know, to think of something nice to say. Because it doesn't matter. Both the chalupa and the taco were so sincerely awful, a food thinking so outside the bun, that I can't even praise the few chunks of tasteless, if still possibly a little healthy, tomato.

But putting that all aside—I know, but putting all that aside anyway—there is something uniquely American happening because of the Taco Bell phenomenon. The people working there describe exactly the diversity of the American culture, even as the economic accident it is, which creates a public workplace where a Mexican national who speaks English poorly works with a nerdy white kid and a honey-talking black woman, where the manager, with two young children, might be named Jim or Ernesto or Tamiqua. And so what if this food's no more Mexican than a hamburger is from Hamburg, Germany—lots of people think it is, and if they think they like Mexican food, and then they want to try tacos at real Mexican restaurants, they may learn that they like not only the food but Mexican people and Mexican culture. That is not how it has been in even the recent past. It represents a positive when other American people might come to understand how *American* Mexican Americans are—seeing that mom and her three sons talking, laughing, eating the same bad chalupas as they do and not knowing any better. It's an Oprah's Book Club bringing culture to the dinner table—OK, so maybe to the coffee table in front of the tube, or maybe through the driver's window and spilled onto the car seat.

Taco Bell's seasoned ground meat isn't *picadillo* because it isn't Mexican. The taco, and its filling, is American now. Like spaghetti really isn't very Italian, like potatoes are not only for the Irish, like French bread isn't French, like a kosher dill pickle isn't only Jewish anymore, a taco from Taco Bell is what food from Mexico can never become because of its variation and specialties in different regions not only on the other side of the border but even on this, the American side: burritos, huge in popularity and girth in California, are exotic in borderlands Texas and New Mexico, while breakfast tacos, craved by all who live in a city like San Antonio, go virtually unheard of from El Paso to Los Angeles. Taco Bell's non- or panregional taco crosses every state line and carries across the country an idea, if not the reality, of an American culture that comes from Mexico. It is, in other words, an American food. Tacos in those crackable, mass-produced shells (which Mr. Glen Bell claims to have pioneered, if not patented), purchasable in sealed, airtight plastic, sold in grocery stores in Maine or Montana, are now no more ethnic than pizza, than a submarine sandwich. Tacos are as everywhere as hamburgers and hot dogs, hot-and-sour and soy sauce, ketchup and salsa. This is an American taco born into a culture without any relatives in Mexico or in the borderlands anymore, that mispronounces a few words in Spanish the same as it does a couple in Italian or Greek or German.

And Taco Bell's success is not only as an implosion of a not very healthy glop, but has to have been the commercial inspiration of at least two new regional fast-food chains—Taco Cabana in Texas and Baja Fresh in California—which dare to feature what would have once-upon-a-time been an exotic, *Mexican* Mexican taco. And that fusion of Mexican culture and the healthy hippie—which bloomed sunflower big into a demand for a nouveau gourmet—is transforming the architecture of food in the Southwest and Texas. In Austin, for instance, where Bush lost big-time in 2004, menus posted outside chic restaurants bear Mexican dish names as stylized as if they were French- or Italian-influenced. And what was unheard of when Mr. Bell first ate plate #3, Mexican restaurants themselves, owned by Mexican immigrants who stay near the cash registers and in the kitchens, no longer look to hire petite waitresses from Tamaulipas or Monterrey but tattooed, slacker-hip white dudes who wear ball caps and cool T-shirts and say "dude" at various times as part of their personalized service.

One last thing, just for the record. That freaking "chalupa" is not a *chalupa*! The word "chalupa," like the word "taco," draws up a specific, historical image and it's one that does not look like a taco any more than it does a chili dog or a steak sandwich. If any old Mexican word can be attached to Taco Bell's latest creation, they might as well call it an enchilada. Enough of the customers won't know any different, most won't care, and in time restaurants will have to explain what those items on a plate that used to be called enchiladas are. Since this chalupa doesn't have Mexican corn in it, why not name it after a Spanish dish, like paella, an exotic name there, or, like a car, give it the name of a famous Spanish city, like Toledo, maybe with a little vowel variation on it, so it might be called a Tolido Taco. Or take it on like Mrs. Bell would. Something like Taco Perro.

Selected Bibliography

Abarca, Meredith E. *Voices in the Kitchen: Views of Food and the World from Working-Class Mexican and Mexican American Women.* College Station: Texas A&M University Press, 2006.

Anzaldúa, Gloria. *Borderlands/La Frontera.* Introduction by Sonia Saldívar-Hull. 2nd ed. San Francisco: Aunt Lute Foundation, 1999.

Esquivel, Laura. *Between Two Fires: Intimate Writings on Life, Love, Food, and Flavor.* Translated by Stephen Lytle. New York: Crown, 2000.

Esquivel, Laura. *Like Water for Chocolate: A Novel in Monthly Installments, with Recipes, Romances, and Home Remedies.* Translated by Carol Christensen and Thomas Christensen. New York: Doubleday, 1992.

Flores y Escalante, Jesús. *Brevísima historia de la comida mexicana.* Mexico City: Asociación Mexicana de Estudios Fonográficos, 1994.

Lambert Ortiz, Elizabeth. *The New Complete Book of Mexican Cooking.* New York: HarperCollins, 2000.

Long-Solís, Janet, and Luis Alberto Vargas. *Food Culture in Mexico.* Westport: Greenwood Press, 2005.

Paterson, Kent Ian. *Hot Empire of Chile.* Tempe: Bilingual Review Press, 2000.

Pilcher, Jeffrey M. *¡Que vivan los tamales!: Food and the Making of Mexican Identity.* Albuquerque: University of New Mexico Press, 1998.

Pilcher, Jeffrey M. "Tex-Mex, Cal-Mex, New Mex, or Whose Mex? Notes on the Historical Geography of Southwestern Cuisine." *Journal of the Southwest* 44 (2001).

Pinedo, Encarnación. *Encarnación's Kitchen: Mexican Recipes from Nineteenth-Century California.* Edited and Translated by Dan Strehl. With an essay by Victor Valle. Berkeley: University of California Press, 2003.

Rivera, Guadalupe, and Marie-Pierre Colle. *Frida's Fiestas: Recipes and Reminiscences of Life with Frida Kahlo.* New York: Clarkson Potter, 1994.

Stavans, Ilan. *Q&A: Latino History and Culture.* New York: Collins, 2007.

Index

About the Editor
and Contributors

EDITOR

Ilan Stavans: Lewis-Sebring Professor in Latin American and Latino Culture at Amherst College. Author: *The Hispanic Condition* (1995), *On Borrowed Words* (2001), *Spanglish* (2003), *Love and Language* (2007), *Gabriel García Márquez: The Early Years* (2010), and *What Is la hispanidad?* (2011, with Iván Jaksic). Editor: *The Oxford Book of Jewish Stories* (1998), *The Poetry of Pablo Neruda* (2003), the three-volume set of *Isaac Bashevis Singer: Collected Stories* (2004), *Becoming Americans: Four Centuries of Immigrant Writing* (2009), *The Norton Anthology of Latino Literature* (2010), and *The FSG Book of Twentieth-Century Latin American Poetry* (2011).

CONTRIBUTORS

Meredith E. Abarca: Professor of English at the University of Texas in El Paso. Author: *Voices in the Kitchen: Views of Food and the World from Working-Class Mexican and Mexican American Women* (2006).

Laura Esquivel: Mexican novelist. Author: *Like Water for Chocolate: A Novel in Monthly Installments, with Recipes, Romances, and Home Remedies* (1992), *The Law of Love* (1996), and *Between Two Fires: Intimate Writings on Life, Love, Food, and Flavor* (2000).

Dagoberto Gilb: Professor of Creative Writing at Southwest Texas State University. Author: *The Magic of Blood* (1993), *The Last Known Residence of Mickey Acuña* (1994), *Gritos* (2003), *Woodcuts of Women* (2001), and *The Flowers* (2008).

Fernando Mendoza: Professor of Pediatrics at Stanford University School of Medicine, Palo Alto, California.

Kent Ian Paterson: Journalist. Author: *The Hot Empire of Chile* (2000).

Jeffrey M. Pilcher: Professor of History at The Citadel, South Carolina. Author: *¡Que vivan los tamales!: Food and the Making of Mexican Identity* (1998).

Encarnación Pinedo: Nineteenth-century chef. Author: *Encarnación's Kitchen: Mexican Recipes from Nineteenth-Century California* (2003).

Helen Simons: Co-editor: *Hispanic Texas: A Historical Guide* (1992).

Frederick Trowbridge: President of Trowbridge & Associates, Inc.

Camilo José Vergara: Photojournalist. Author: *The New American Ghetto* (1995), *American Ruins* (1999), *Subway Memories* (2004), and *How the Other Half Worships* (2005).